JUNGLE MAN

The Autobiography of

MAJOR P. J. PRETORIUS

C.M.G. D.S.O. *and* BAR

With a Foreword by

FIELD-MARSHAL J. C. SMUTS

With Photographs and Maps

E. P. DUTTON & COMPANY, INC. ⟋ *New York* ⟋ *1948*

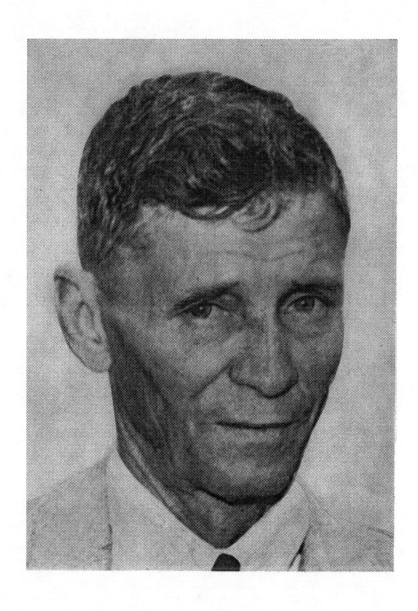

The Author

I dedicate this book
to those staunch young friends

RAOUL LE SUEUR

AND

PHILIP PRETORIUS

who, with me, spent many a pleasant
evening round the fire while on Safari

Foreword

I GLADLY WRITE a foreword to this amazing book. If it were merely a work of fiction it would be a remarkable achievement. But it purports to deal with matters of fact, and to relate a true story, and that adds immensely to its interest. The tale of continuous adventure for a lifetime which it records is surely one of the most extraordinary ever written. I have never seen a more thrilling story of a hunter's life. It is full of almost unbelievable incidents, of reckless daring, and of hair-breadth escapes. If one knew the writer the interest increases, for he was a quiet, gentle, unassuming person in appearance. What fire lay hidden under those quiet features and that gentle manner! His very person seemed to be a camouflage.

Major Pretorius was the chief scout to my forces during the East African Campaign. I had not known him before, and I first heard of him towards the end of 1914 when, as Minister of Defence in the Union, I received an inquiry from the War Office about a certain Pretorius who had been an elephant-hunter in German East Africa. It so happened that he had just arrived in the Union from East Africa, and was actually under observation as a suspicious character, possibly an enemy agent! He was wanted by the Navy to assist in finding the whereabouts of the German cruiser *Königsberg*, which had sunk the *Pegasus* at Zanzibar and then gone into hiding in the Rufiji delta. In this book Pretorius gives the first full account of the search for the cruiser and of its destruction, and anyone reading it will agree that it is a first-class story. But it is

7

only one of innumerable thrilling incidents with which this book is crammed.

Subsequently, when I took over the command in East Africa, I found him in the Intelligence Service there, and I soon had reason to convince myself of the unique quality of the man as a scout. I had learnt the business myself in the severe school of the Boer War, and could therefore judge of the real article when I saw it. And so I gave him a free hand to carry on in his own peculiar way. Thin, lithe, and colored brown from continual bouts of malaria, he looked more like an Arab or a Somali than a European. With a band of native askaris he would roam about the enemy forces and behind their lines, in close contact with the natives, and with his own men continually mixing with the enemy askaris and unsuspectedly gathering information from them. At many critical junctures he would thus supply me with invaluable information, as readers will see in this book.

While his war service as a scout was outstanding, and his story in this connection is both interesting and deserving of close attention, most interest will be taken in his experiences as a hunter of big game. Here he seems to have found his best self-expression and to be the true artist. Indeed, one has the impression that he became a great scout among men because he was the supreme scout among wild animals. Courage, coolness in facing up to danger, extreme resourcefulness in emergencies, a singular combination of dash and caution, acute observation, and a sense of realities which is unanalyzable and amounts to instinct or genius — whatever name one may give to it — these are the qualities that go to the making of the great hunter and the great scout alike. Pretorius possessed this combination of qualities, and hence was so distinguished both as hunter and scout. Repeatedly in this book he speaks of occasions when without any apparent reason he had a warning sense of danger which turned out to be well founded. Thus, in

Foreword

quite a different field of activity, Socrates had his warning dæmon on grave occasions. This endowment is given to some and can never be acquired by others. It is in the nature of a sixth sense. In Pretorius we have apparently such a case of insight far beyond the ordinary, and taken in conjunction with his other qualities it led to a life experience in many ways unique, and to a book which I for one have found of enthralling interest. I commend it to all lovers of fine qualities and great experience.

J. C. SMUTS

Editor's Note

GENERAL SMUTS in his foreword refers to the unassuming character of Pretorius, and I think it should be stated here that if this intrepid hunter had followed his own instincts he would never have set down in writing his romantic adventures. Fortunately, before his death in December, 1945, a friend, Mr. L. L. le Sueur, who knew something of his exploits persuaded him to make the notes from which this record has been compiled; otherwise one of the most intriguing life-stories, with its fascinating new light on the jungle life of man and beast, would have been lost to the world.

HAROLD WIMBURY

LONDON
August, 1947

Author's Note

UNFORTUNATELY at the outbreak of the first World War I was in German East Africa, and this entailed the loss of treasured photographs and records. Consequently a number of photographs appear in this book which were taken many years after my various excursions, but which will help to give some idea of the country and its inhabitants. To those who have so kindly gone to such trouble to help me out of this difficulty of suitable illustrations I tender my most grateful thanks.

Finally I find myself at an utter loss to express the depth of my gratitude to Mr. L. L. le Sueur of Johannesburg, who some six years ago suggested that I should write the story of my life, and has given up most of his spare time for the past eighteen months to sorting out and verifying the material.

P. J. PRETORIUS

NYLSTROOM
July, 1939

Contents

Illustrations

Maps

Jungle Man

CHAPTER ONE

Lifting Horizons

LIVING dangerously is twice blessed — it blesses the moment with elation; it blesses the after-day with warm memories. If a man has trodden unknown trails and landed on lost beaches, when age comes the domestic hearth is a campfire where old dramas are relived.

I must have been born with the divine unrest of adventure in my blood. I should have wilted in a town; even the open and active life of a South African farm, which was my home, seemed to "cabin, crib, and confine" me. My immature imagination pictured all Africa spread around that homestead, and I wanted to lift my horizons. When I was thirteen my father, trading horses and cattle with the natives, took me on my first long trek into King Khama's country. From that moment nothing could have stayed me from a wandering life; it was at that time I planned to walk Africa from end to end! Since then for half a century I have hunted every type of big game; have known scores of native tribes, speaking their language, living their lives; have trodden jungle paths not used before by civilized men but made by the animals of the forest through countless years. I have stalked the rhinoceros, the lion, the bush-buck, shot hundreds of elephants (five on one occasion that were charging down on me in a bunch), and made friends with natives who had never seen a pale-face.

I have stalked men, too — men who were England's enemies. And once it fell to my lot, at the request of the British Navy, to stalk a cruiser — the famous *Königsberg*, which, after its

17

raiding exploits, had scurried for shelter. As on other hunting trips, on that memorable occasion too we made our kill.

All the facts of that historic chase are given here in print for the first time, and the exploit perhaps makes a fitting start to the tales I ask you to share now the camp-fire is lit and the day falls. Incidentally, the *Königsberg* adventure typifies a period of my life the recollection of which brings a special glow, since it was then I left for a time the shy paths of the forest, where hitherto I had spent the years, to serve under that gallant soldier-statesman who is now Field-Marshal J. C. Smuts, P.C., C.H., K.C., Prime Minister of South Africa.

Even then, though amid an army, my task was still a lone one. For the scout follows remote ways. It was like a diver coming up for a breather when I returned to headquarters with my cap full of news after expeditions into enemy territory.

But before my life as a scout with Smuts came the episode of the *Königsberg*. This enemy warship had left a spectacular trail of disaster behind her as she ploughed those southern waters. She had sunk merchant vessels and transports and had ended by smashing up H.M.S. *Pegasus,* as well as two guard ships. Then she scurried for shelter, for her commander knew the British Navy would be out to get her as surely as, much more recently, another German commander — the captain of the *Bismarck* — after the sinking of the *Hood,* was well aware that ships flying the White Ensign were gathering from every direction like hounds round a trapped quarry.

The Navy knew where to look for the *Bismarck,* but in 1915 the Admiralty had no definite information as to the where-abouts of the *Königsberg*. They thought she was hiding some-where on the east coast of Africa and suspected the Rufiji delta, a desolate region of river swamp and jungle. It chanced that I had hunted there and was one of the very few white men who was familiar with the country and the natives.

Thus it was that — without knowing at the time the reason

for it all — I was brought by urgent message, the mystery of which intensified as I was swept onward across the continent from Pretoria to Cape Town and Durban, and put aboard the battleship *Goliath*, on which Admiral King-Hall flew his flag.

I remember the *Goliath* put to sea with me aboard amid luxuries to which I was not accustomed and which contrasted violently with the previous quarter of a century I had spent almost entirely alone in the wilds.

I had been brought aboard by the Captain himself, had been sumptuously fed, and to the thrum of distant engines lay and wondered at the strangeness of events. Here was I, descendant of the famous Voartrekker general who gave his name to that Pretoria I had quitted eight days ago, and son of a Commandant who on two separate occasions had waged war against the English, now a guest of the King's Navy.

I had always been a loyalist. Back in my youth I had seen service with the forces of Rhodes's Chartered Company and, only just prior to the present adventure, in my home country of the Transvaal, had dispersed a smouldering rebellion. I had fought against the Germans and been wounded in the first month of the war. But as the great ship throbbed through the darkness that night it was natural I should be consumed with a tantalizing curiosity, for I had, as yet, no knowledge why I had been picked up from among my small private affairs and whisked on to a man-of-war. It seemed a long jump from my usual life of hunting, where, if I had a war, it was one of my own against such foes as the fierce Mashukulumbwe and the Congo cannibals, or against the animals of the jungle deeps.

However, I was to see the Admiral in the morning.

King-Hall was a charming man, slightly under six feet in height, red-complexioned, and possessing the bushiest eyebrows I had ever seen on a man. From the very first I instinctively liked him. He shook hands with me and signalled me to sit down.

"Pretorius," he commenced engagingly, "do you know that I am the ugliest man in the British Navy?" He seated himself in a chair alongside me, and said: "Now I will tell you what we want you for."

Then he explained he was after the *Königsberg*.

He told me they thought the ship was up the Rufiji river, and their chief evidence seemed to be the loss of searchers that had already been sent out there. Two seaplanes had flown over the delta, and neither had returned. Two armed whalers had been dispatched to patrol the coast. One of these, armed with machine-guns and light cannon, had entered the river and had not come back. Finally the Navy had sent an ordinary boat filled with local natives, but this too had disappeared.

The Admiral had a scheme to construct a raft substantial enough to carry guns as well as men, and on this he proposed to penetrate the delta; but that looked like suicide to me — if the Germans were there. So far as anyone knew the cruiser's powerful guns and her torpedoes were undamaged. And she might be lying sixteen miles from the coast-line, since the main channel of the Rufiji — called the Salali — is deep. Sixteen miles of approach through swamps and streams dotted with small islands offering innumerable opportunities for ambush!

I suggested that, with a few natives, I should go scouting, first of all to discover whether the *Königsberg* were indeed there, and then how circumstances could best be used to attack her.

Twenty-two miles off the mainland in those parts lies an island called Mafia, and there the Admiral landed me with a staff of one — a wireless operator. It's not a big spot, roughly twenty miles by eight miles, but fertile, producing coco-nuts, the plantations run by Arab and Swahili labor. It had been a German outpost, but on January 11, 1915, had been shelled and blue-jackets had captured it. It would make a good base for me, and I knew of another "two-by-four" island, named

Koma, only a couple of miles from the river mouth, which would serve as an F.O.P.

Just as I left a wireless message was received from Whitehall asking how long I estimated it would take to ascertain whether the enemy ship was in the delta or not. I guessed about eight days. And eight days it was.

A Colonel Mackay, of the King's African Rifles, was Resident Commissioner of Mafia, and he helped me pick my assistants, assuring me cheerfully that the six I eventually chose were the biggest rogues on the entire east coast, but adding that they made up in courage what they lacked in morals. I preferred fearlessness to any fastidious taste in native honor, and I assured myself of their silence by the threat that wagging tongues would be cured by removal. I spoke their language well enough to carry conviction.

I had been promised that if I buzzed an SOS help would arrive immediately, all ships having been warned, and I must say that throughout the rather lengthy and tricky operation that followed the Navy's arrangements were so perfect that I could call up a ship almost with the ease one whistles a taxi.

Two days after I landed at Mafia I "whistled" and got an immediate reply from H.M.S. *Weymouth*: "Will arrive 3 P.M." When night fell I "taxied" across in her to the mainland with my company and a large dug-out, which had to be shipped aboard because the sea was too rough to permit of towing.

It was a hectic scramble getting from ship to shore at Koma. Not a soul was on the island; all the villagers had been cleared out. Why? This was the first support to our suspicions that the German ship was in the neighborhood. The islanders might give them away, so the Germans had removed them; that was the logic of it.

Next night — dark, wet, thundery, and therefore friendly to spies — we pushed off in the canoe for the mainland. I knew a village near the coast — Kisiji — and I planned to adopt the forthright stratagem of knocking on the first door and capturing anyone who emerged. But in this I was frustrated. For there was no inhabitant left in Kisiji. But if there was no tongue to speak, this little ghost village told its own story. The Germans had cleared the coastal region to prevent the natives from talking. Apparently their logic didn't embrace the fact that the very act of removing these people implied there was something to move them for.

There was nothing for it but to penetrate farther inland, and we returned to our forward base until next night, when we crossed again, meaning to stay until we had results. So this time we hid our dug-out among the mangrove-trees where we landed. Not that "landed" seems quite the right description, for there is no ground visible at the edge of a mangrove swamp. These trees grow from the sea-bed up to the water's surface, where they spread out so densely that one can scramble over the growth. We had a full mile of this unpleasant route to traverse from the edge of this sea forest to dry land. It was raining heavily; it was pitch dark, and I dared not light a torch.

We made a bee-line for the west, so that the next morning we should be among the native population, and there I decided I would stay until we had captured a man who could impart useful information. At about 3 A.M., after having travelled eight miles, we struck a big, wide road which had obviously been made since the outbreak of the war, for I knew these parts well and remembered there had originally been only a native footpath there. Taking up our position in very dense bush beside the road, we lay down for the rest of the night.

In the morning I noticed that the road was used almost hourly during the day by German troops marching backward and forward between Dar-es-Salaam and the Rufiji river. The enemy was here of a surety. At nine o'clock a very large safari of porters carrying supplies to the Germans on the Rufiji passed us, but there were too many of them for us to tackle. Eventually two local natives came along. I told my boys to stand ready, and as they came up I arrested them, took them into the bush about five hundred yards, and there questioned them.

I told them right from the start that in no circumstances could they be released for the duration of the war.

"You will be prisoners, but you will be kept and well fed," I said; "but at the first sign of treachery you will both be shot." Then I asked them for information concerning the German cruiser. They answered that it was in the Rufiji.

"We will go to the *Königsberg* to-night," I said, "and you must guide me to a high point as near the cruiser as possible, where we will remain for the rest of the darkness, so that when it gets light I shall be in a position to see the ship and the German forces."

They replied that there was a small hill close by from which the *Königsberg* would be visible; we could climb trees and sit in them until the day broke.

When daylight came the quest was finished. From a tree-top I had a bird's-nest view of the cruiser, which lay moored not more than three hundred yards away. She was well camouflaged, smothered in trees on her deck, and her sides painted so that she seemed part of the surrounding jungle.

There were patrols about, and we had to be wary in returning. Not until dark did we reach the dug-out at the edge of the mangrove. Before daylight we were safe at Koma with our two prisoners.

Orders had been given to the Navy that during my absence from Mafia one ship was to patrol the coast-line every night to ascertain when I wanted to return, and it was arranged that I should light oil-soaked sacks on the beach away from the mainland as a signal that I wished to be picked up. Everything worked to plan, and we were taken to Mafia, where "Sparks" sent out a prearranged signal, "Pretorius wishes to see the Admiral," which he knew meant that I had found the *Königsberg*. "Will arrive 10 A.M. to-morrow" came the prompt reply.

King-Hall was on time, but not in the *Goliath*. During my absence the Admiral had hoisted his flag on the *Hyacinth* while the *Goliath* was sent to Egypt: and we learned later she ran across a mine in the Red Sea and was sunk with the loss of many lives.

I found in the interview witn tne Aamirai that the locating of the ship was but the preliminary part of my job. Weeks of scouting lay ahead. He wanted to know the range from the sea to where the *Königsberg* lay, what guns she still possessed, whether her torpedoes were aboard, the rise and fall of the tide in the main channel and certain subsidiary streams. It all came back to me when listening to Mr. Churchill's broadcast picture of what complicated strings had to be pulled in order to draw in the wide net to entrap the *Bismarck*.

King-Hall was leaving nothing to chance; when he struck he meant to kill, and so, while his fleet steamed off on their own concerns, I set about my further plans. Thus a few days later I wirelessed a call for the ship to pick me up, and this time the cruising "taxi" turned out to be a giant Cunarder, the *Laconia*.

When darkness fell we put out from Mafia, not a light showing, every port-hole closed, the crew under orders not to strike a match or smoke a cigarette, and we quietly approached our F.O.P., landing on Koma in the dug-out. Next night, with one of the prisoners as guide, we dodged all German sentries, and before dawn had crept to the vantage-point from which, as soon as daylight came, I could look down on the *Königsberg*. Through powerful glasses I could see the guns and the German sailors, brought so close, it seemed, that by stretching out an arm I could touch them. I counted eight 4.1 guns. This was one item of information the Admiral required. I had already one other — I had found the distance from ship to sea was seventeen miles. Now I had to discover whether the torpedoes were aboard, if the various channels had been mined, and the depth of water at high and low tides along navigable routes. British charts contained no data regarding the Rufiji delta.

I had a scheme which my personal acquaintance with the natives made possible of execution. A few miles inland lived a certain chief who, I thought, could lead me to the knowledge I wanted. The Germans had recruited native labor, and through the chief I might make contact with a boy working on the ship.

It had scarcely ceased raining all the time I had been engaged on this mission, and it was pelting as usual a few nights later as I sat in the bush outside a native village awaiting the return of my prisoner, whom I had sent to fetch the chief. I heard them approaching, and I am afraid the act I contemplated was a very unfriendly one. The moment the chief stood before me I collared him. He took his capture stoically enough and, indeed, seemed pleased when I told him that, though he could not return, he would be paid five pounds a month plus all rations. He was also delighted to know the British were around, promised entire secrecy, every collaboration, and even to go back home for half an hour in order to kill five Germans who were in his village making a general nuisance of themselves!

When he knew what I wanted he replied excitedly that his own son was a stoker on the *Königsberg*, and he said if one took a basket of chickens it was possible to visit a relative who was a member of the crew. He offered to go to interview his son, and I said I would go with him.

For this purpose a disguise was necessary, and the chief provided me with an Arab outfit. I needed no coloring; twenty-five years of African sun had provided that.

The chief was to pose as my "boy," and we had many rehearsals, especially as to what exactly he should ask his son, for it would not do for me to interrupt their talk with the Germans looking on.

Came the day when we sallied forth on our adventurous mission. Near the raider's hiding-place one of the pickets stopped us, and behind him I observed lines of tents where the sailors were lounging, since they lived ashore. The slightest suspicion on their part, and our chances would be nil. However, we were letter-perfect in our parts, and humbly I explained that my "boy" wished to see his son for a few minutes and that I myself was on my way to Mahoro, at the same time offering the basket of chickens. The German went off and reported the matter to an officer. When he came back he told us to sit down, and that in a few minutes he would send the son to us.

A quarter of an hour later the boy arrived from the *Königsberg*, sat down, and was interrogated by his father in accordance with my instructions.

"Where are the long bullets that swim in the water?" That was the chief question. The boy stated that the torpedoes had been removed from the cruiser and, he believed, placed in boats close to the mouth of the Rufiji river. I was later informed by captured Germans that this was perfectly true. They were ready to be fired at any British ship that might approach the entrance of the Salili.

This was vital information for Admiral King-Hall, who, when I gave it him, ordered all shipping to keep well out to sea when near the Rufiji.

It appeared later in the German Press that as soon as the *Königsberg* had emplaced torpedoes ready to fire at British cruisers the enemy men-of-war vanished, and the Germans accused one of their officers on the ship of being a traitor.

Meanwhile Admiral King-Hall instructed me to find a possible channel of approach to the *Königsberg*, and to locate a suitable range-point in the delta.

And here began a series of investigations the monotony of which was only bearable because of the results gradually obtained. I pushed a dug-out in and out of the score of channels, taking sounds with a long pole, often risking daylight in order to map the localities, perhaps glad of the relieving sense of adventure brought by the possibility of a Teutonic face suddenly peering at me out of the bush.

It was in the most northerly channel that I eventually found what we wanted. For seven miles the pole revealed no obstacles and an uninterrupted six to seven feet of water. Then I came upon a solid reef running across the entire channel effectively blocking progress. I knew that the possibility of bringing over monitors then being used on the Belgian coast had been considered, if they could be got within range. So I walked the distance between this reef and the German ship and found the range not too far for six-inch guns. And a monitor has a draft of only four feet. When I returned with the news the Admiral at once requested that two monitors should make the long trip from the English Channel to the coast of East Africa, while we watched that the quarry did not escape in the meantime.

Then I was given a simply ghastly job. I was instructed to stick a marked pole in the sea a certain distance from the shore, and for a month — *one month* — make an hourly record of the rise and fall of the water with the ebb and flow of the tides. I'll say I was glad the day I placed the chart in the Admiral's hands.

In due course monitors arrived — the *Mersey* and the *Severn* — and I was signalled to come aboard the flagship, where I received a good many instructions, the chief object of which seemed to be to try to lure the *Königsberg* into the open. It looked very much as if a couple of dhows I was to commandeer were to be the lure! If that were the object it failed, for a storm got up and we lost each other, one dhow disappearing, the other, in which I was, being wrecked during darkness on one of the countless reefs that lie between Mafia and the mainland. We struck about a mile from the mainland, and about three miles from a German outpost from which I and my crew of askaris would have been clearly seen the next day. Fortunately, the following morning the tide was out, and I found we were strandard half-way between Koma Island and the mainland. Soon a small steam launch appeared, and as it approached I saw it contained Germans. We promptly undressed, jumped into the sea, and made for Koma Island. We should have fared badly, only by good chance, when up to our necks in water about three hundred yards from our wrecked dhow, one of our whalers, under a Captain Wood, rounded the island and picked us up, the enemy hastily retiring.

I did not know what had happened to the second dhow, but one thing was pretty certain: the Germans knew we were on their track. Any doubts about that were dispelled the following night, when once again I made the journey across those mangrove-trees and on to the hill overlooking the *Königsberg*. Dawn showed me our missing dhow tied up beside the warship; and the following night as I returned (having hidden in the bush all day) I overheard Germans discussing defense works.

Back on Koma Island, I informed my boys it would be desirable for us to make investigations and find out exactly what these people were doing. I explained that we should go right inland again, and hide there for a day or so until we found some one who could ascertain what actually was happening. Each of the boys was given one pound in small German silver, and I told them that if during the night on our way past the suspected place any of us should be intercepted by an enemy outpost we should all scatter in different directions. Any who escaped would then be able to live among the local natives, using the small change to buy food. If this happened the person or persons escaping were to look for an opportunity to steal a boat and put out to sea. I also explained that during the eight days we should be away a Navy ship would be patrolling up and down the coast, so that any boy who managed to reach the sea would be picked up.

We started off at nine o'clock from Koma Island. It was raining heavily again, and this time we did not hide the dug-out in the mangroves but beached her ashore. I gave instructions to two boatmen that they were to remain where we landed for an hour, and if after that no firing was heard they could return to the island until time to pick us up.

The three boys and I landed, but we had not gone more than five hundred yards when we heard shouts from all sides commanding us to stop! We started running in different directions, and the enemy at once opened fire. There was a tremendous commotion. We heard orders shouted to shoot first at those running down to the sea — myself and one of the boys. They chased us all the way, firing the whole time, the noise we made going through scrub bush in the dark giving away our whereabouts.

At the landing-place we saw that the boat had already started for the island, but luckily it was only about forty yards out to sea, so we rushed into the water. The boat stopped and backed, and we managed to scramble aboard.

The whole German line stood on the sand and fired volleys, but the darkness saved us, and we arrived safely on the island. There I signalled in the usual manner, and Captain Wood came to pick us up.

I told him that two of my men were lost in the bush, but I was hopeful that they would not be captured as I had given them instructions to steal a boat and make for the sea.

We commenced a hunt, and for four days sailed up and down the coast with a man in the crow's-nest to keep a look-out, but we saw nothing. On the point of giving up the quest, the man aloft broke our long disappointment with a sudden shout: "An object in the water right ahead."

Captain Wood took his telescope, and at once picked it up — a dot on an empty sea, which, however, as we approached, gradually materialized into my two boys in a boat. They had no oars and were steering with a piece of wood from a paraffin box. One of them stood in the prow holding up a stick about four feet long on which they had tied their loin-cloths, which acted as a sail. They were nearly all in, having been drifting two days and nights without food and water.

On that occasion I had nothing helpful to report, but the need for secret scouting was over. The fight was on. Our whaler was to be used as a decoy, and a few days later, running under sealed orders, Captain Wood and I opened an envelope the Admiral had given us as we put to sea. It was midnight, and we were instructed to come to anchor at daybreak at a spot marked on a chart. That spot was right in front of where I knew German batteries were fixed close to the shore.

But we were not alone for long. Backed by an angry dawn, we began to count smoke smudges on the horizon — sixteen of them. Our job as temporary watch-dog was over, and I felt a new thrill at the thought of the naval action that was impending — the first I had ever witnessed.

The flagship came to anchor opposite us, and the Admiral signalled for me to come aboard. In the meantime the two monitors steamed past on our port, led by two mine-sweepers. I was watching their slow progress towards that position I had found for them, when right between us the sea seemed to burst and a tremendous column of water shot up into the air in front of the flagship, followed by a thunderous roar that filled the world. The *Königsberg* had opened hostilities, and that single shell was quickly followed by others, while the land batteries also began to bombard us.

The two monitors held on their course without firing a shot.

Photo *South African Railways and Harbours*

"When out of the water to feed he opens his enormous jaws" (see pp. 40-41)

"The Zambesi teemed with crocodiles" (see p. 59)

But our ship came to life. Orders were sung out to the men already at their stations, and our guns spoke. We fired in salvoes, all previous noises fading to insignificance as salvo after salvo belched out. It was terrific — to me — and I gaped in wonderment at the nonchalance of the English sailors. One group, not engaged in the firing, were calmly sitting on the deck mending their boots, and others were stitching canvas just as if nothing untoward was happening. They did not even trouble to watch the bombardment.

Although the officers were using field-glasses, I was able to point out to them a number of snipers placed high up in trees on platforms whom they had not observed. Once spotted, the snipers were wiped out immediately, platform and all.

The firing increased, and now it burst out from a new quarter in the very heart of the bush. The monitors were in action.

Two aeroplanes had appeared over the delta, and I was informed signals were being received from them.

"Fire again at the same mark." This they kept sending over; it meant the monitors had found the target. They were using incendiary shells which burst into flame as they landed, and we soon saw a dense cloud of smoke rising, a hopeful sign that the *Königsberg* had been hit, although we could not see her because all the firing was indirect, over the hills and bush.

The fighting continued until about two o'clock. I was standing beside the Admiral behind one of the conning-towers where the wireless messages were coming in, and the chart I had made during that month of investigation was lying beside him on a table. It told him to the minute how long we should be able to remain in our position, and here was reward for that month of monotony.

The Admiral finally gave the word for all the ships to raise anchor and put out to sea. Orders were spoken, the telegraph sounded, the engines throbbed — but the *Hyacinth* was stuck.

Had the Admiral delayed too long? Was my chart somehow at fault? It was an anxious moment. The engines raced and stopped, reversed and raced again, and finally the ship slowly dragged herself forward. A few sluggish movements and then she was off, released.

"Enter in the log-book that the flagship grounded for five minutes," calmly remarked the Admiral to the Flag-Commander.

We regained the open sea, and the firing ceased. It began to rain again, and there was a dense mist. For six days, since the mist lasted that long, we did not know what had happened to the enemy, save that he was mute.

At length the rain stopped, the mist cleared. Out of the murk the outline of the mainland emerged slowly. It was with mounting curiosity that our landing-party made for the river. Unmolested, we penetrated to where the enemy lay.

The great ship's devastating career was ended. One would scarcely have known what she had been. For here, beside the bush-crowded edge of the small island against which she had been moored, lay little more than a vast disorder of tortured steel, made the more unlovely by broken bodies strewn at every angle.

It lies there in the Rufiji to this day.

Whenever in these present momentous times I read some laconic paragraph indicating that the Navy has attacked and sunk some enemy ship, I wonder how much scheming and dare-devil courage have gone to achieve that three-line result. In uncounted cases no one outside the few men concerned will ever know.

This brief account of the *Königsberg's* end may offer a small ruler with which to measure them.

CHAPTER TWO

Frontiers of the Unknown

MEMORIES are pictures, and they form haphazardly on the mental screen. Thus, as I contemplated setting down some of the experiences that have come my way, it chanced that the day I have just described, when we stood in the silent African bush looking at the burned and contorted mess that had been the *Königsberg*, came first in my recollections.

Now others crowd, bringing scenes of encounters with wild animals and wilder men, of aching hunger and the madness of thirst. But none linger in my mind more abidingly than the crack of a whip that sounds across the years. It represented utter freedom for me — the first time I was trekking on my own, all the magic world before me.

I can still see a long train of wagons, drawn by trek-oxen plodding over the sandy plains of Bechuanaland and Southern Matabeleland, raising great clouds of red dust, struggling on and on through the thorn bush and the stunted forest growth to the next outspan. In my ears the cracks of the long whips, the shouts of the many natives who accompanied us, and the rumbling and jolting of the lumbering vehicles.

As the sun sinks, a red globe of fire over the western lands of the semi-desert, we halt for the night, if water is available. Soon great fires are burning, the smell of wood-smoke and the savory scent of a buck cooking in the pot greet our nostrils. After a crude meal, devoured with the appetite and zest of hard-worked youth, the natives sing and jest, some one produces a concertina and plays songs and lullabies. Then, healthily and comfortably tired, I wrap myself in my jackal skin (kaross) and sleep the sleep of the man of the veld, whose ceiling is the stars.

I was sixteen, and my father had sent me to ride transport for the British South Africa Company, which had been formed by Rhodes — founder of Rhodesia as we know it — in 1889. The famous Lobengula, king of the Amandebele, was then (1893) putting up a fight, so that there was constant danger of our wagons suddenly finding themselves in the centre of a scrap. But soon the savage king fled, and the new king — Cecil Rhodes — reigned. That dreamy Englishman, who thought in terms of continents, arrived in Bulawayo two davs before I reached the capital of Matabeleland.

I went a good many journeys with the wagons, out a terrible outbreak of rinderpest killed off so many oxen that transport was brought to a standstill. Trips dwindled, and, to cap my troubles, my parents insisted on my returning home. I didn't want to go, and said so. Their representations brought me before a magistrate, and he ordered me to go back. But the uneventful life of a Transvaal farm held no attractions for me. I had to move on, however; so, with other transport riders, I set out in the opposite direction — for the Portuguese frontier, via Mashonaland.

It was twenty-five years before I saw my parents again.

On transport we arranged that as many wagons as possible should journey together, for the country was in a state of war and it was unsafe to travel in small parties. We trekked from Fort Victoria through the Makalaka country (before any roads had been made), where we pushed a tortuous way past kopjes and big granite boulders that looked as if they had been piled up on top of one another, with an occasional swamp to add variety. It was tough going with the cumbersome wagons. But it was a grand life, and my ambition that, one day, I would penetrate into the deeper wilds, grew. Though it was to be a year or two before I was really foot-loose and on unknown trails, the hope to go went ever before me, lanternwise. But an expedition required preparation, and meanwhile I had to live. I achieved one dream when I pushed off alone to Umtali; and even if I passed through a malaria belt the resulting pains did not damp my ardor.

Truly my knowledge of tropical hygiene was negligible. I knew, however, of one drastic but efficacious method of combating fever, and this I practiced. First of all, I made the tent or hood of the wagon perfectly air-tight by stretching a large tarpaulin over it, and then a pot filled with water was put on the fire to boil. Inside the air-tight tent two powders, "witfametif" and "grauwfametif," were swallowed, followed by nearly a gallon of very hot water. Excessive vomiting resulted. It was a crude and unpleasant method, but effective.

In due course my wagon rumbled into Umtali, and I pressed on to the Portuguese border at Macequece, which was the rail-head of the line that was advancing from Beira, twisting and winding through the great Amatongas Forest, to open up the new land. Railwaymen were busy on construction work; surveyors rigged their theodolites and peeped through spaces in the bush. What a toll of life that railway took!

The first day after we left Umtali we arrived at an outspan, where we noticed six dead natives lying alongside the road. We inquired from other natives as to the cause of the deaths, and they told us they did not know, but that it was a very bad sickness, because a man would become ill in the morning and be dead at night. In two days we must have seen at least fifty corpses lying along the road at the outspans. When we reported the matter to the Portuguese they sent out a number of native police. They simply dragged the bodies into a heap with the aid of a hooked stick, then carried big piles of wood, which they placed on top of the bodies, and set light to the bonfire, letting the pyre burn until flesh and bone were completely incinerated.

35

Jungle Man

At Macequece there was plenty of transport work offering again, and I had another spell of it. This time it took me to Salisbury, where fighting was going on. My adventurous spirit led me to join in. I was small for my age, did not look more than fourteen, and therefore evaded a recruiting office for fear of rejection. Instead, I proceeded to the military camp and had a general look round. While regarding the Maxim guns, I heard two Tommies in conversation saying that they were going to the Hartley Hill district. I asked whether I might go with them, and laughingly they declared that they were sure I would be a great asset to the army. They signed me on, and here I was in my first war! It was an irregular procedure, but, in those days of confusion in Rhodesia, irregularities were more often the rule than the exception.

The very next morning we broke camp. After three days of trekking Captain Rhodes, brother of the great C. J. R., spotted me sitting on the Maxim. To him I must have looked a small, forlorn figure — a Kim, indeed, perched on the gun of Zam-Zammah. He asked the gunner who I was, and, to my great delight, said that he would see that I was properly attested. Thus I became a full-fledged trooper of the British South Africa Company's forces.

The column marched throughout that day, heading for the village of a big chief named Machangombe. Our route lay through treacherous country, in which were caves and kopjes that could have sheltered thousands of natives, and a sharp look-out had to be kept for ambushes. The Mashona showed signs of hostility, and the next morning we attacked the village, where the natives put up a stout fight. This was my baptism of fire, and it was here that our C.O. noticed my extraordinarily good eye-sight, and saw that I was able, with the naked eye, to spot everything long before those who possessed field-glasses. I was also a good judge of distances and so, despite my youth, I was elected to act as guide.

After some skirmishing we drove the enemy into a cave, and compelled them to surrender by dynamiting their refuge. Hundreds of natives then poured in to surrender. We remained stationed here for six months, during which time the fighting ceased. The campaign over, I asked for my discharge, and set off for Salisbury wondering what was the next step towards my ultimate goal. I made for the gold belts.

My knowledge of mining was confined entirely to accounts given me by old prospectors. I had a natural aptitude for languages and soon spoke various different native tongues, a qualification of no little value on a mineral property where large numbers of "boys" were employed. On arriving at the Chicago Gaiko Mine I soon got a job, and there I stayed for eighteen months, working in various capacities. I held on in order to save enough to equip that expedition I yearned to take into the wilds, and as soon as I could I bought a .303 rifle, a few hundred rounds of ammunition, a tent, and about a hundred pounds' worth of trading goods — unbleached calico, brass, wire beads, and so on. North of the Zambesi, I understood, money was not known, and my idea was to exchange these trading goods for foodstuffs. Then — at last! — I set the prow of my ship of fortune in the direction of the river of romance — the Zambesi.

That journey from Salisbury to the Zambesi in 1899 was not commenced under the happiest of auspices, for the rainy seasons had commenced. But my ambition to traverse Africa along unexplored routes was so strong that climatic considerations counted for naught.

At first I set my course in a westerly direction and tramped through dense bush and scrub, onwards to the beckoning mountains. It was hard going in this range. I do not think they had previously been traversed by a white man, because for several days I saw no evidence of a felled or blazed tree. Progress was slow, and as one ridge after another was surmounted

I would look back over a wide panorama of bush-robed kopjes, spurs, and krantzes, fading away to plains grey-blue in the distance.

After one day's long trek I pitched camp near a stream in a pleasant open spot. My boys went to carry water and returned in great alarm to say that they had seen the tracks of a very big animal. I examined the spoor and was unable to recognize it. While I was wondering what it was one of the boys shouted three or four times, and on looking round, to my alarm, I saw a rhinoceros within twenty yards of me, emerging from the thick bush. The beast charged through my trading goods, and after I had fired two shots he went back the way he had come. I followed, keeping him within range, and firing shots whenever I had the opportunity. After a while the rhino looked backward and lay down. I was then able to approach within fifty yards of him and try to get a shot to the brain. My other cartridges had been hastily fired and were badly placed; but before I fired again the rhino rolled over dead. This was the first large animal we had encountered on our trip, and as the boys were eager for meat I selected a steak for myself, instructed the chef-boy to cook this well, and told the other members of my caravan to help themselves. But that steak was uneatable; it tasted more like rubber than anything else. Among all big-game flesh I think the rhino is the only animal whose meat is useless, although the flesh of the water-buck is also very unappetizing.

There were in the country no footpaths of any description except rhino paths, which must have been there since time began. By following these tracks I climbed for miles in comparative ease, so well were they selected.

Among the many wild animals found in this mountainous country were baboons, and I had many opportunities of observing their habits. The baboon is an amazing creature; his instinct for danger is as uncanny as his wariness in regard to poison. I could take two apples, cut a hole in each, put poison in one, cover up both holes again, and throw them to a baboon; invariably he would eat the good apple and reject the poisoned fruit.

A baby baboon, only a day or two old, knows immediately that the danger of a scorpion lies in its tail, and, if he catches one, will first of all break off the tail and throw it away. Baboons apply this same wary sense to wild fruits and underground plants. They always know which are poisonous and which are not, and anyone wandering in the veld may without risk eat any berries which these creatures devour.

This part of the country had never been inhabited by any native race; it was weird and lovely, without a trace of habitation, a true no-man's land. There were no attractive camping spots, and for ten days while we were in the range rain fell continually and drenched us to the nethermost skin. This lasted — until, from there being too much water, there was too little, and we became parched. There is no longing in the world like the mad wish for water, when the throat goes gritty and the tongue swells, when one cannot swallow. This is torment, stark and unforgettable.

We were so tormented that we discarded our loads and went in search of water. From the plateau where we were we looked down on to a valley, and a line of large trees apparently outlined a river. We raced down, but found only a dry river-bed. While we were bemoaning our ill-luck a bush-buck jumped into view. I fired, the buck dropped, and we hastily drank its blood.

We continued searching throughout that night for water, and towards midnight heard the barking and scratching of my dog — he had found water in a cleft of a rock. It was a little pool, full of leaves, and the liquid had a terrible smell, with the appearance of strong tea, but we strained it through grass and distributed the water among us, the dog included.

And then we discovered, quite near, a large pool of fairly clean water, round which rhino spoor was much in evidence. So the awful spell ended. We had fresh meat and water, and for two days remained there. The memory of those days will never desert me, for only those who have suffered acutely from thirst can realize its tortures.

After our sojourn at the large pool I returned to recover my equipment, which fortunately was intact. Now another misfortune befell me; my boys revolted against going any farther. This uninhabited land, with its waterless stretches, had shaken their nerves. They could not, however, have re-traced their steps to the villages unless I went with them — since without me to shoot meat for them they would have starved — and I determined to press forward. Alone in an unknown land, with the nearest white man hundreds of miles away, I had to take the law into my own hands. A few cuts of the sjambok inflicted on the ringleaders of the mutiny served to bring the porters to their senses, and my caravan started northward again.

A temporary reward met our next stage of the journey, for, after we had ascended another plateau, as far as the eye could see there appeared to be an enormous expanse of water. My boys gleefully shouted, "The Zambesi," and I too thought we had reached the river. Here my caravan rested for the night, but next morning to our consternation there was not a sign of a river; what we had imagined the previous evening to be the Zambesi had been a thick mist lying between two mountain ranges!

We now commenced the descent of the escarpment. It was difficult and trying work, and we often had to retrace our steps to find a way to the plain below. When we were about half-way down I distinctly heard what sounded like the banging of an empty tin just below us in a big kloof, or ravine; at last we were again in touch with human life. I had been told that if natives saw us unexpectedly they would run away into the bush and we should never see them again, so I decided to encircle them. Continuing our descent, we presently came upon five natives. Sure enough, as soon as they saw us they ran like wild animals; but we managed to capture two, and I was able to follow their language, which was a dialect of the Makalaka of Southern Rhodesia. As we had been living on meat for a fortnight, I was most anxious to establish bartering relations with a tribe with whom we could trade. I therefore asked my captives to direct me to their chief, and this they agreed to do on condition that they ran ahead and informed the head-man of my arrival. The natives showed me a path which ended very quickly in thick, dense bush, and I realized I had been duped.

We were all ill of dysentery from the continued meat diet, and it was essential to split the safari into two parties. It was agreed that the first to sight the village was to light a grass fire, as a signal that the native huts were found. After walking for about two hours we observed a mahobohobo tree. I was gathering fruit on the higher branches of this tree when I heard the yells of a child. I descended the tree, and, running in the direction of the screams, came face to face with a party of native women. As I was the first white man they had ever seen they fled into the bush, but we pursued and caught them. When they heard me speak their language they soon lost their fear and agreed to conduct us to their village, which was six miles away on the Angwa river. On arrival I found that the habitation was of fair size, and that the land was cultivated. These natives, however, lived in a state of semi-starvation, and depended to a large extent on the wild fruits which they gathered. The old chief, a villainous-looking individual, told me that the Zambesi was a good five days away, so we decided to rest here for a while.

Since I had left the outskirts of Salisbury this was the first

village I had seen. It was not at all a prepossessing place, and
the tribe was about the poorest and the filthiest lot of natives
I have ever seen. At night cattle, goats, men, women, and
children were all herded together in a large kraal, and, as can
be imagined, the stench was atrocious. When he chooses the
site of a village the first thing a native looks for is its position
with regard to the most suitable spot for tilling lands. The
village is built in almost any locality, and questions relating
to hygiene and sanitation scarcely enter the heads of the
designers.

Where we were a variety of game was to be found in the
surrounding bush — water-buck, sable, antelope, and small
gazelle, but no elephants. Each morning while we remained
I shot one or two buck to provide food for my own boys, and
for the village people. It was here that I shot my first lion.
That is a very definite picture in a hunter's memories.

Lions can be dangerous enough when they mean business,
but I do not hold them in such high regard or esteem as
elephants, of which I have shot 557.

I had left the filthy little village and was following the tracks
of a water-buck when suddenly I came across the great pad-
marks of lions, firmly indented in the soft ground. I traced the
spoor down to the river-bed — where signs of a characteristic
struggle between wild animals were seen, showing plainly that
the great tawny cats had attacked the water-buck and killed
it. I followed the lions, and, after a long hunt, came right on
two of them, lying fast asleep. I shot one and wounded the
other, which made off into a near-by ravine densely covered
with reeds. We could hear him grunting in this undergrowth,
but we were unable to reach him, and, after spending a whole
afternoon waiting for him to bolt, we went back to the village.
Returning the next morning to continue the hunt, we found
that the lion had vacated the ravine and had made off towards

the south. We found him about two miles away, along the river-bank, dead.

Hyenas were very ferocious hereabouts, so much so that the old chief urged me to build a zareba (hedge) of thorns round my tent He said that a hyena would enter a hut and maul a sleeping man's foot if the door was left open. There was, he declared, no danger of the hyena killing a man, but at night these beasts were exceedingly bold and cunning. I found out later that these stories of the hyena were true, for I often saw natives who had not only their heels torn away, but sometimes a whole side of their face.

After remaining at this village for a week we started off for the Zambesi. The old chief told me of the existence of a white man somewhere along the river. Although the head-man of the village had never seen this somewhat mystic personage he appeared to know quite a lot about him. The presence of another European here, in this remote part of the world, intrigued me, and I made up my mind to visit him.

We had our first view of the Zambesi river when we were still fully two days' march away, and on top of a high mountain. We saw a line which looked like mist, and indicated the flow of the noble river. It is beyond my powers of description to make anyone realize our joy when we knew we were within reach of the river, for we had been marching in quest of it for six weeks. Then one day we burst through the bush and saw the Zambesi scintillating in the sunshine almost at our feet. The first great river of my dreams.

CHAPTER THREE

Savage Zambesia

I REMAINED IN ZAMBESIA for more than three years. There were a good many occasions when anxiety sat beside me, an uneasy companion. For the inhabitants were strange people, all suspicious, and many hostile; and, if I went in as a youngster of twenty, I came out a man, considerably aged by strange experiences.

I caught a first glimpse of the aborigines as we came to the river — they had spotted us and scurried for their canoes, and we just saw them disappearing out of sight. For days they made no sign. Night hours were ever pregnant with the possibility that they were watching with unfriendly eyes. Most of them had probably never seen a white man before, because at the time of which I write it was uncharted country, often resounding to tribal fights and the screams that accompanied slave raids.

Then one morning I came across their footprints not very far from our camp, and, following them, discovered a bit of ground they were cultivating. It was obvious that they had been crossing the river daily to do their gardening — and my suspicions that we had been under observation were substantiated. I determined to make contact with them, and, since they were so shy, the only way was to pounce. So my boys and I lay in wait and captured two of them. What followed seems amusing now, but at the time considerably piqued my juvenile pride.

When my prisoners heard me speak their language they responded and seemed friendly enough, so I asked them to bring their head-man, who, they said, was the Paramount Chief Mburuma. The chief refused my invitation, but sent a canoe to fetch me. I didn't hesitate, and crossed to the other bank, where my guide led me to the bole of a big tree, and there left me. Presently I saw a very big man, with a large escort, emerge from a hut. He was smoking a huge pipe and wore a magnificent leopard-skin kaross. I naturally expected him to come to me, but, instead, he walked right past the tree where I squatted, ignoring me completely. He sat down about twenty yards away — with his back to me! After a further lapse of time, to add to my rising sense of humiliation and anger, he sent one of his men to bring me to him.

Chief Mburuma had an impressive beard, several inches long. He was very tall, well built, and of an upright carriage. The pipe he smoked consisted of a calabash a foot long. The bowl was of pitch-black polished clay, and was beautifully carved with heads of wildebeests. After his childish display of independence he talked, and, sitting there in the shade, away from the burning sun which made his skin shine like an advertisement for boot polish, we had a lengthy indaba. I was thrilled at one fact he mentioned, as though one of the "great ones" of history suddenly strode across our little savannah. . . .

"I have met other white men," he said. "My eyes saw the man Livingstone when he passed this way."

But he had no use for us. He wanted no pale-faces in his country. He had fought several who had come down from Portuguese territory. In the end, however, I persuaded him of my peaceful intentions, and we became friends. He took my gifts, and I accepted his invitation to hunt hippos. This proved an exciting game, which, by the way, was by no means a one-sided affair. The hippopotami often took their toll of life. The hunting was done from canoes — long, narrow, treacherous boats, with flat bottoms. As many as thirty canoes may take part in a hunt. These assemble under the dense shelter afforded by the undergrowth on the river-bank. When everything is ready the order is given and the canoes are released. The hippo immediately dives, for he knows from previous experience that he is being hunted. The animal can stay below for only about ten minutes, and the leading canoes shoot over him in quick succession carried by the swiftness of the current. When the hippo comes up to breathe a harpoon is thrown. The accuracy of aim is remarkably good, and the hunters seldom miss the mark. The harpoon need penetrate no more than one and a half inches below the hide. The rope drags along with the harpoon, and remains floating on top of the water showing the position of the beast as he viciously thrusts his head under water. The hippo then commences jerking the harpoon; presently he becames infuriated, and frequently attacks the dug-outs. As the amphibian rises to attack more harpoons are cast; five at least are required to hold him. The harpoons are then pulled in, and assegais, with blades two feet long and five inches wide, are employed to give the *coup de grâce*.

When a boat is attacked the occupants jump into the next one. If the hippo actually secures a boat he very soon destroys it by crunching and tossing it into the air like a bit of match-wood. As soon as the animal has been dispatched he is dragged into shallow water. Before the cutting up commences the medicine man arrives, walks round the animal three times, repeating incantations, and then points to the different parts of the beast he requires. The natives without a murmur cut off all the tit-bits for the privileged witch-doctor, and the remainder is then divided.

Hippo-skin makes excellent eating if boiled down to a jelly. The carcase is cut into small strips, and a wooden platform is erected near the hippo; the meat is then cured — hide and all. In appearance hippo-meat, if allowed to bleed, is just like beef, the grain being very fine. It is, and has always been, my favorite dish, but, of course, it is essential that it should be fresh. The fat is invaluable for cooking purposes. I defy anyone to detect the difference in taste, when it is rendered down, between it and the purest lard. Four gallons of fat can be obtained from one animal.

The method of hunting hippo at night is to sally forth with one or two boys and travel against the wind; it is impossible to see the animal at any distance, but he is easily located by sound, even five hundred yards away. When out of the water to feed he opens his enormous jaws, and his worn tusks grate one against the other making an easily identifiable sound. On one of these night hunts the animals were located in fairly deep water, and I undressed to approach them. Suddenly I came right on a hippo — I could see the outline of his head. Then I did a foolhardy thing; I decided to try a spine shot with my .303 rifle. I succeeded in wounding him, and he swerved, whereupon I found myself with my prey between me and the shore. The hippo splashed and submerged me, but then made off. It was lucky for me that I never saw him again.

I was made free of the country, and came to know many of the people, hunting and fishing with them. I was so lost to the "civilized" world that I never heard of the Boer War until it was all over!

Slave raids were quite common. These were carried out by Portuguese and Asiatics from the east coast. Even today it is a custom when any stranger appears in a village for the headman at once to warn neighboring villages. This habit emanated from the slave-trading days, when it was obligatory for one village to warn the next, so that the inhabitants had the opportunity of escaping into the mountains and evading capture.

When a raid took place, and the slave-traders captured a number of people alive, they did not take the old, although sometimes the aged and infirm were killed. And those who were carried off were threatened with death if, when they came to a more or less civilized country, they informed anyone that they had been taken into bondage. I have on many occasions come into a village where a slave raid had been in progress, and found that invariably it was a fight for life. The occupants of the huts defended themselves with bows-and-arrows, assegais, and knives, but if an opportunity occurred they took to their heels and endeavored to escape to the mountains. During these raids cruelties were naturally rife, and I saw some poor creatures with great gashes in their heads, and others beaten almost to death.

There were two methods of manacling the captives. One was to cut sticks about two inches wide and six feet long, with a fork at the end, each fork being fourteen inches long. This yoke was placed on the neck, with another stick in front, and was fastened with a rope. I think this was the most merciful method of binding the slaves together. The other way was by tying the hands. When this was done, the ropes were drawn so tightly that the circulation of the blood was stopped; the hands swelled, and great pain resulted.

The raiding was unusually done at night. The capitanos who were in charge of them were often called upon to prove their honesty in these bartering transactions. They had to prove that they would keep neither the goods nor the slaves (and especially the young girls) for themselves. The Indians and the Arabs I knew used the native form of trial when there was any doubt on this question. And this was the manner of the trial: a large clay pot of water was placed on the fire, and the accused had to dip his hands in the boiling liquid. If the skin was not badly scalded the accused was proved innocent.

I have witnessed many native trials. Frequently a herb called mafia (a small scrub) was used to establish innocence or guilt. This herb, when boiled, is a very potent purgative. A strong dose of this is administered, and if it has no effect the man's innocence is considered to have been established. If a man is accused of adultery and found guilty he is proclaimed an outlaw and is driven into the bush. He is unmolested for a day or two and given a fair chance of escape, but thereafter the first man belonging to the tribe who meets him is at liberty to slay the outcast.

In the case of a woman found guilty of breaking the seventh commandment the punishment meted out was entirely at the discretion of the husband. He had paid for his wife, she was a valuable chattel, and consequently the punishment nearly always resolved itself into a severe thrashing; after which the woman was sent to take her place in the fields with the others. The old proverb of "A woman, a dog, and a chestnut-tree, the more you beat them the better they be," must, I think, have emanated from Central Africa, as it is there put into practice so conscientiously.

The natives of Zambesia knew of a number of poisons. If a man was to be killed secretly the conspirators employed a parasitic plant, called karatonga, which has the appearance of a scarlet runner with very few leaves. Karatonga grows plentifully in the dense undergrowth of thick bush, and the bulb is anything from two to three pounds in weight. This bulb was taken and the outer rind peeled off; after this it was cut into thin slices and dried in the sun. The slices were then ground into a thin powder. When prepared it was given in kaffir beer — and one dose was fatal.

At the time when I first knew these natives they had never come in contact with the white man, and the chiefs were in complete control. It struck me as being very strange to find that they had an unshakable belief in spirits. Their creed was that if a man became ill, and no remedy known to them proved effective within a few days, the "Mazimu" was calling him;

the spirit of some ancestor was endeavoring to communicate. In such a case a beer-drink was ordered. The relations made all preparations for this, and when ready beat the drum, the sound of which carried for a distance of ten miles. There were recognized intonations of the drums for burial, war, "Mazimu," and so on. I attended one, since everybody was welcome at these rites. When the people were gathered together they sat on their haunches in a circle, and the sick man was placed in the centre on a mat. The singers commenced to chant their threnodies, and on this occasion for hours there was no change in the comatose condition of the invalid. It became rather boring. Eventually, however, the sick man started to speak in an unrecognizable voice, as if he were in a trance. There was then absolute silence. The trance-voice began to make complaint about the distribution of his goods, and the relatives discussed the matter in all seriousness, adjusting the matter. After the instructions of the "Mazimu" were carried out the sick man recovered. It was almost biblical, the way in which he rose from his bed and walked, and I was assured this nearly always happened. It sounds unbelievable, but unbelievable things happen in African deeps.

Speaking of illness, there were scores of quaint — and some quite efficacious — methods adopted by these savage people. Once I was suffering from a particularly bad dose of fever and had to be carried in a machila, or hammock, to the nearest village of a big chief, named Katumba, on the south bank. About six miles from the village we noticed something floating down the river; it looked rather like a bundle of rugs tied with rope. The natives with me were greatly excited at the prospect of acquiring blankets from an upset canoe, and dragged the bundle into the boat. Upon untying it, however, they found, to their horror, that it was a native man dead from smallpox. Hastily they threw the gruesome find back into the river. On arrival at our destination we discovered that smallpox was rife; and it was there I first witnessed their crude treatment of this dread disease.

Smallpox is not apparent at once in natives; for a few days they will have all the appearance of fever, and when the spots first appear these resemble ordinary mosquito bites. A native will remain in isolation until the spots are all out, and at this stage the patient is taken to the river-bank, stripped, and placed in the sand. Then the roughest bark available is rubbed into him, until all the inflamed and pus-filled sores are broken! This, of course, causes excruciating pain, and often the victim has to be held down by a number of men. When there is no longer an unbroken mark on the body the unfortunate sick man looks a ghastly sight. He is then led into the river up to his neck, and is washed clean. The treatment is certainly drastic, but in recommendation of it I may say that I did not see a single pock-marked native during my sojourn in Zambesia.

Another remarkable fact I discovered was that these natives, achieving by instinct what science has taught to civilized folk, had a primitive form of inoculation. When a smallpox patient reached the stage where suppuration was at its height all the natives of that district were called together, with the medicine man in attendance armed with an iron-bladed knife, the handle of which was usually made from the tusk of a hippo. He took the left arm of the person to be inoculated, and severed one of the arteries. With his knife he then drew the pus from the sick man, injected it into the artery, and stitched up the wound with twine made from bark.

While I was in that district recovering the epidemic of smallpox was entirely eradicated in a few months.

Natives living near the Zambesi river follow the usual South

Central African custom of burial, by digging a grave and placing the dead man in it, together with all his worldly possessions — clothing and ornaments and spears. Then follows a tremendous ceremony. Hundreds of natives from the surrounding villages gather together in full war-dress, ornamented with skins and feathers plucked from large birds, such as the marabou stork. They descend upon the village of the deceased, and when about ten yards from the entrance charge with poised spears, shouting a war-cry and yelling in a truly blood-curdling fashion. Three times they rush through the streets of the village whooping, and generally succeed in frightening the children out of their wits. Then they depart homeward.

One of these macabre stampedes took place on an occasion when I was in a village and knew nothing of the burial which had taken place the previous day. The inhabitants were alarmed, as an invasion had taken place the day before, and they imagined this to be another raid. I grabbed my rifle, and was prepared to protect myself and my boys from the shelter of a hut, when one of the inhabitants realized that it was only a death parade, and pacified my alarms.

Concerning their customs, I was always amused at the way they arranged their marriages. Formalities were brief, and the ladies had little to say in the matter. They didn't even have to say "I will." They just had to agree willy-nilly, as long as the suitor — or should I say the claimant? — paid the price. And that wasn't high!

When a man desired a girl he went to the parents' hut and left a goat (there were no cattle in this district). This action spoke for itself, and the girl was immediately handed to the man, who took her away with him. Should a man not be able to afford a goat it was enough if he collected as a marriage gift a large bundle of firewood, weighing anything up to a hundred pounds. The wood had to be cut into small lengths of about three inches and tied firmly with rope. The firewood was placed at the doorway of the parents' hut, and the girl required was delivered to her lover. There was no wedding ceremony of any kind. The business was almost as free from difficulties as among the animals or the birds.

CHAPTER FOUR

War in the Bassouri Country: A Memorable Lion Hunt

THE truly magnificent scenery of the Zambesi Valley seemed a most suitable background for the big game that abounded, and as one passed through the jungle deeps one constantly came upon their spoor, heard their voices, or unwittingly, almost stumbled on them. With this abundance of quarry, and incursions into unexplored country inhabited by hostile tribes, there was excitement and to spare.

I shot scores of elephants during my stay there, chiefly with the object of obtaining ivory to barter for supplies and equipment. Down in Zumbo, where I had to go for these, money was unknown, and ivory was a useful means of exchange. I could get down to the place in a couple of days, but it took sixteen to pole back up the Zambesi. So on the return journey I would send boys in charge of the boats, and return overland through Kanyemba's village, and round the mountains of the gorge. This allowed me to enjoy wonderful hunting — elephants, buffalo, and rhino, besides every kind of antelope. No more enticing hunting fields could be found on earth.

At one village I heard of two species of antelope which were to be found on the opposite bank of the Kafue — the Sitatunga and the Lechwe. The natives warned me of the difficulty and danger of crossing; for at that time of the year the river was in full flood, with many little islands of floating trees, branches, and grass. Eventually two natives agreed to accompany me in a small dug-out, and advised that we could cross the Kafue above the rapids. It proved a fateful trip. At a point where the river was about two hundred yards wide, with a very swift current, the boy who was paddling was unable to make the other bank, and we were swept towards the rapids. I had been in too many tight corners to panic, but that day I certainly thought my last hour had come. Fifty yards above the rapids, however, I noticed some trees projecting above the water. We were swirling broadside towards certain death, and the boys paddling the canoe, abandoning all hope, had sat down in blank despair. It was time for quick thinking and rapid action, so I decided to make a jump for the trees, and, leaping like a springbok, managed to secure a grip. The boys awoke from their lethargy of despair and followed me, and, perched there, we watched the boat go racing over the rapids.

We had to stay on our precarious refuge until late in the afternoon, when, fortunately, a woman appeared on the bank. She ran to the village to obtain assistance, and presently people came with another small dug-out. They secured this with a long piece of rope to the river-bank and floated it out to us. We climbed in, and were drawn back to the mainland. It was a touch-and-go affair.

A day or two later I made the crossing in a large canoe, and it was while hunting over there that I learned of a tribe called the Bassouri, who lived in the north-west. I was told that they were a fighting race, and would not allow any strangers to pass through their country. That was the sort of challenge which, in those days, was irresistible to me, and I pushed on to meet the Bassouri.

I was refused permission to pass through the country by the first outpost I encountered. They declared the chief would not in any circumstances permit me even to interview him, so I was compelled to remain on the fringe of the country for two days, in the hope that the chief would come to see me — I did not know at that time that the potentate himself was in the party who had met me on my arrival.

When I realized that there was no chance of proceeding,

and saw how terrified my boys were, I retired for a distance of ten miles; then I struck out in a more northerly direction. This brought me to another large village completely enclosed by stockades. Here the chief accepted the usual presents, but refused an interview, and demanded that I should pitch my tent in the centre of the enclosure. This message was brought by a head-man with an escort of sixty warriors. I observed that this head-man had one cheek missing, and learned later that he was a celebrated hunter, and that the facial mutilation was the result of an encounter with a buffalo bull. I also ascertained that the so-called head-man was the chief himself, and that his name was Chibalo, but he never acclaimed himself to a stranger. I decided to take the chance, and entered the stockade. The following day I was not interfered with when I set out to shoot game for the pot in a beautiful country, green and open, with plenty of water. I had to travel some distance before I found buck and was overtaken by dusk, so I made for a village I could see in the distance. I had a feeling that trouble was brewing, as all the natives I saw were armed with assegais and bows-and-arrows, and scores of them were hiding in the fields of kaffir corn. I sent two of my boys to call them to come into the open, as I wanted to speak to them; but they refused, and I realized they were bent on capturing me. I got away into a clear space on the open veld, only to find that hundreds of men and women, beating drums, were advancing on me in half-moon formation. My natives, with the exception of the cook, who loyally remained with me, took to their heels and disappeared.

I endeavored to convince my potential antagonists that I was on a friendly visit, but I could see that they intended to encircle me, and I was presently forced to fire at their feet to keep them at bay. That halted them temporarily, and, taking advantage of their disorder, we managed to evade them in the kaffir corn. Darkness was falling, and the Bassouri were now ahead of us, marching for the camp with their war-drums and horns creating an awful din. Fearing that the natives would head us off, I took a circuitous route, and about half a mile farther on noticed, on top of a hill, a hut outlined by the light of a big fire. I was bitterly cold, and decided to take risks for warmth. I found two stockaded huts, and entered one of them, when suddenly a man appeared with a bow-and-arrow, and threatened to shoot me. I covered him with my rifle and drove him into the hut. Half an hour later I reached camp and found my tent intact, but none of my natives were there. A fire burning some little distance away showed in its light people dressed in European clothes. I was amazed, and rushed to them. I found an Indian, who, on seeing me, clasped his hands together, and in poor and terrified English told me that we were all to be killed. Even while we talked natives surrounded us on all sides, climbed on to the stockade, and shouted that we were to be killed the next morning.

I called the Indian and his boys and rushed for the gates, firing shots as I went. I succeeded in forcing an exit and then found I was alone. Wondering what had become of the others, who were nowhere to be seen, I trekked on into the night and presently came to a small kopje. Here I whistled, and suddenly my cook appeared. He had not seen the rest of the party; but after travelling for another half-mile we whistled again and obtained an answer from three members of the Indian's party. They said the Indian and themselves had found a hole in the stockade and had escaped through this, but they did not know what had happened to the others.

Next morning we reached the summit of a big range running from the west side of the Zambesi, and travelled the whole day without observing a sign of the hostile natives. So excited had we been that we had not realized our hunger. But a native cannot last as long as a white man, and at the end of the second day my boys were famished, declaring that they could proceed no farther. We managed to find some beans to stave off hunger, but my natives said they would rather die than proceed, and one of the Indian's porters actually did collapse and die. After a great deal of arguing I persuaded the boys to climb one more mountain range.

"We shall then see the Zambesi," I encouraged.

This gave them hope, but they were so weak that we advanced in very slow stages. Eventually we reached the top of a mountain, and from there, as the sun was sinking, I saw the Zambesi in the distance. But we were so feeble from fatigue and hunger that each step forward seemed like a league, and the river was fifteen miles away. Presently we came to the Kafue river, where we found a field of kaffir corn. We ground some grain and made porridge, but after swallowing a small quantity my natives and I became violently sick — in consequence, I suppose, of having had no food for four days since our escape from the hostile tribe. Had we died on the mountains we would never have been discovered, for the range we scaled had never been crossed; for all I know it is still unexplored.

We arrived at a village, but found to our dismay that it was deserted — an ominous sign of raids and warfare. My boys became frightened, and insisted on retreating into the bush; but just after leaving the deserted huts we saw smoke rising from a little island in the Kafue, and I decided to shout and make my presence known. Immediately two natives replied, and paddled across to us in dug-outs. They said that two days ago they had heard that I and my boys had been killed, and along the Kafue they had been threatened with extermination, for permitting my party to pass through their country. In anticipation of an attack they had fled.

We crossed over to the island, and here observed a number of half-grown chickens. One of the natives instructed his wife to kill a bird, and, although I thought I could have eaten three myself, I told her to make soup of it, which she did; and this, together with a pot of porridge, we all shared. I could stomach the soup, but the porridge made me ill again. It was nearly two months before I recovered from exhaustion, hunger, and sickness. Then I proceeded to Zumbo, in Portuguese territory, in order to obtain supplies, and on the way down I hunted freely. Licenses were unknown in this no-man's land, and I could shoot whatever I desired.

Unfortunately, I was unable to obtain ammunition at Zumbo, and eventually I had not a single cartridge left, so I made up my mind to proceed to Salisbury. Before I had gone many miles I came on the spoor of a herd of zebra travelling in the same direction as ourselves. We followed the tracks for about a mile, and observed the spoor of lions following the zebra. Soon I saw that the lions had killed one of them, and close by we came on the killers — four of them lying quite peacefully, while the fifth was tearing out the zebra's entrails.

We advanced to within fifty yards of the lion, who merely stared at us. This was the first time I attempted, unarmed, to take away the "kill" from a lion, but we wanted meat badly, and I therefore told one of my boys to follow me and help drive the lions away. Then I maneuvered, not proceeding in a straight line towards the lions, but moving as though I intended to pass them. When I had gone thirty yards a lioness arose, and climbed on to the bank. The other lions followed her, and when they were on the top looking around I ventured nearer, then made straight for the zebra and took possession of the kill.

I expect they were all overfed, or they would have had more to say in the matter.

After a ten days' trek I reached Lomahundi, a police camp, where I was able to obtain cartridges. It was on arrival here that I first heard anything about the South African War, and was told it was over!

Possessed of ammunition, it was unnecessary to go on to Salisbury, and we returned, along the route we had blazed, to the Zambesi. I have described this trip, not only as indicating the life I was leading, but by way of introduction to a most exciting, not to say extremely fortunate, lion hunt. At Urungwe, on the return journey, I met an old prospector who was on his way to Salisbury. I had a Martini-Henry, and he a .303 sporting rifle. He asked me to exchange, and, as he had more ammunition for his rifle than I had for mine, I agreed. I was soon to realize that I had made a bad bargain.

One morning, I saw from their tracks that seven lions had crossed our path during the night, and were travelling in an easterly direction. There had been heavy rains, and the spoor was easy to follow, so I told my boys to pitch my tent and wait, while two of them and I followed the lions. At length I came up with them; they were lying sleeping on a large ant-hill, about a hundred yards from me. With the two boys I crept to within fifteen yards of the beasts, where there was a big tree, and when I was beneath it I loaded my rifle. The two boys climbed the tree, while I took careful aim at a beautiful black-maned lion. The rifle misfired! Luckily the lions were asleep and had not heard the click of the rifle. I pulled back the bolt and shot again, and this time the cartridge exploded and the lions stampeded.

With us we had a native mongrel dog, which rushed after the lions, and one of them charged it. The mongrel ran straight back to me, and the lion dashed after the dog until he was about ten feet off, when he stopped and crouched, facing me. The dog had dashed past and run off. I took aim, and pulled the trigger. Another misfire! And yet another! I was defenseless. I knew if I attempted to run I was doomed, so I stood stock still watching the lion, which, suddenly, to my intense relief, changed its mind in regard to killing me, and with a mighty roar loped off to join its friends.

I opened my rifle, threw away the cartridges, reloaded, ran after the beasts, and tried to get in a shot, but that rifle misfired yet again! Just as I was entering a patch of reeds I sighted the lions once more, and this time one of my cartridges exploded, and I saw a lioness jump into the air with a roar — a sure sign that she was wounded. She dashed away, and I reloaded and rushed into the reeds, reaching the spot where I had hit her. I found that she had bled freely, there being a large pool of blood about four inches across. I followed the trail with ease, and found her a few yards away, dead.

While I was looking at my bag the boys shouted from the tree to come quickly as there was a lion below them. I hastened back, and to my surprise saw a lion still lying alongside the ant-hill where I first encountered the pride. I could see at once that the beast was dead, and I then realized that my first shot had been effective, but the other lion had charged so quickly that I had not observed what actually had happened to the first. It was a wonderfully lucky shot, for it had penetrated one ear, passing through the skull, and out of the other, leaving the skin without a blemish. I kept this skin, and many people who saw it said that I must have obtained the beast by poisoning; but the bullet mark was quite clear in the skull.

We pitched camp here, and started to skin the lions, which were the fattest I had ever seen. They possessed fat very much like that of a pig, two broad strips of it round the kidneys, adjoining the fillet. We collected as much of this as we could, and rendered it down. At this time the rainy season was on, and we were soaked by abnormally heavy rains. My tent leaked badly. When transport riding I had learned the trick of keeping a tarpaulin waterproof by covering it in fat, and I therefore used the lion lard for this purpose. While we were all busy waterproofing the tent a native passed through the camp. He was carrying a letter to Salisbury, and told us that just after I left my main camp three Europeans had arrived, and had crossed the Zambesi with a small army of porters and a quantity of trading goods. He also declared that one of these men was so ill that he had been unable to continue the journey, and was lying in Mzimu's village.

It is, of course, as much a rule of the wild lands as of the sea to go to the succor of one's fellows in distress, however far it may take one from one's course, and therefore I set out at once on the trail which the strangers had taken. On arrival at Mzimu's village I found a man named Nelson, who was almost dead from a severe attack of malaria, and was unable to move. I pitched my tent, and stayed there treating Nelson until he was strong enough to be carried in a machila, or covered stretcher, to Salisbury.

Jove! but I regretted the fatty waterproofing of that tent of mine. In the hot sunshine it simply reeked, and I had to get the natives to construct a grass shelter for me. It was a good thing I did, as it turned out, for one morning, on going to where my tent had been pitched, I found nothing but pieces of canvas lying all over the place. I searched for the cause, and soon observed the spoor of hyenas. It was fairly obvious these scavengers had been attracted by the stench of the lion-larded tent. On investigation I found they had extracted the fat from the canvas, and left the rest in tatters. Needless to say, I never used lion fat again to render my tent waterproof!

It was not long after Nelson had gone that I received a call for help from the two who had been with him. A letter was brought me by a native which said the white men were stranded. Their boys had deserted, and they were in hostile country. So again I went trekking, and it took me eight days to reach them—McGregor, an Australian, better known throughout the whole of Southern Rhodesia as "One-eyed Mac," and Williams, a Welshman. Hard by was the village of a big chief, named Chirome, and I made friends with him, so that we were left unmolested. I had to thank my reputation in these parts for this. It is, of course, eerie how information seeps through these wild regions, and from tribe to tribe my name had been passed in native lingo. They called me "Mtanda Bantu," and I was pretty proud of it. Its best interpretation is "Friendly with the People." No official passport ever helped a man so well.

Mac and Williams had come north with a lot of trading goods, worth some four hundred pounds, and, in addition to the articles of the usual character, they possessed a large number of rare shells that looked like white jade, and were thought much of by the natives.

They hadn't been able to do much trade. In point of fact, the Mashukulumbwe in the district had refused to let them travel farther — that was why their boys had become frightened and deserted, leaving the two white men stranded — and so now they suggested that I should go into partnership with them, and do the bartering with the natives. I agreed, and, while the others stayed in camp, I obtained porters and made several eight-day trips, soon disposing of all our goods in exchange for cattle; of which, when the business was concluded, we possessed no fewer than four hundred head; and fine beasts they were.

CHAPTER FIVE

Trade, Assegais, and Hunts

In the vast hinterland of untrodden mountain and jungle that spread about my headquarters there were many different tribes, all living just as their ancestors had done for centuries. Writing of first this and then that may convey the erroneous idea that they were all close neighbors. Often I heard of some tribe and, having decided to explore that territory, found myself launched on a trek that lasted weeks. I might do a journey the length of England with Scotland thrown in, crossing rivers, climbing mountains, blazing a trail through dense bush and forest, hunting all the way, not for trophies but for food.

It was while bartering for cattle that I first heard of the Watwa, a warlike tribe living on the water of the Kafue river. I learned that they built their huts on poles above the river, and, naturally, I was interested in the report that much ivory was accumulated in their villages. Having no lands to cultivate, and living mostly on fish and crocodiles' eggs, all of which were handy, they had plenty of spare time to pursue their chief hobby, which was fighting.

I determined to pay them a visit and, hoping that my peaceful reputation might have reached their ears, I sent messages through the bush asking for permission to land on the "island" which was their domain.

Eventually I was granted permission to visit the portal of their territory — in other words, a certain tree standing at the edge of the water. I set out with eight of my natives, and I was armed with a Mauser pistol and an ordinary shot-gun. On

64

"Lions lying quite close to the grazing animals" (see p. 95)

Photo Ray R. Ulyate

"Wild dogs . . . are hated and loathed by all" (see p. 97)

reaching the appointed place we were met by warriors, in ten canoes, who had been sent to conduct us to the chief's village.

Here a rondavel was pointed out for my occupation. It could not be described as a "desirable residence" — the place simply stank. Every roof in that village was covered with rotten fish, and there were flies in millions. The natives' haphazard habit of curing fish was to get them and throw them on the roofs to dry. My boys were sent into the same hut with me, and as we were all very hungry I told the cook to procure something to eat. I did not look outside to see what was happening until I had finished my meal; then I noticed that there was not a single canoe in sight. We were stranded in the middle of the Kafue.

I shouted until I got a reply from a hut on an adjacent island, and asked what had become of the dug-outs which had brought us. The inhabitants said that all the inmates had gone to a beer-drink in a neighboring village, and would be back some time the following day. The next day passed, the flies tormented us, and the stench of the rotten fish was terrible. Crocodiles, attracted by the smell, teemed all round the island, and I was decidedly anxious to get away from this loathsome prison. But I was doomed to be the target of a grim bit of native humor. In the afternoon some natives approached in canoes, shouted that they were not returning, and that I must get back to the land as best I could. Since the water was full of crocodiles one could understand their wide grins. And they went on fooling me like this for several days. Our discomfiture was increased by the fact that we had no wood for fires.

On the afternoon of the seventh day of my isolation in this hellish hut a hundred natives approached in their canoes, each warrior armed with at least three assegais, and landed. What could we do? We were overwhelmed, and everything that I possessed was taken, with the exception of my shot-gun, my pistol, and a small quantity of food. For a moment I considered opening fire on the robbers, but that, I quickly decided, would have been useless, as we were utterly outnumbered, and one shot from the gun would have meant a cluster of spears in our ribs.

So the villainous Watwa departed, and as they left they shouted that they were coming back to kill me the next day. Sure enough, with the morning they returned, and it was tragically clear that there was no hope of escape except by force. I therefore decided to make an attack on the first dug-out that reached me, and told my boys to be ready to help capture a boat, at the same time warning them not to kill unless they were absolutely compelled to do so. When the first canoe came near the hut I jumped into it, and my men followed, among them my cook-boy, Sherakain, with the shot-gun. A dire struggle took place as we pushed the paddlers out. My cook went overboard with my treasured Greener shot-gun, which was never recovered, but I managed to drag him aboard, and we paddled away as fast as we could. The other canoes chased us, and I warned my pursuers that I would kill if they threw a single assegai. They accepted my challenge, and I was forced to fire a few shots right into their dug-out. This checked their ardor, and they kept about forty yards behind, trying to encircle me. But we turned into shallow water, paddling like fury, where I abandoned the dug-out and made a dash for land. The Watwa recaptured their boat, but, for some reason, did not continue the chase. I suppose the joke was over. Anyhow, we lost no time in making for the camp of McGregor and Williams, where I arrived with only a loin-cloth and a gun!

I found McGregor dangerously ill with fever, while Williams was dosing him with quinine, aspirin, and calomel. He complained that his teeth were all loose, and his gums were exceedingly inflamed and sore. He was so ill that we decided to make a machila, and send him back to Salisbury for proper treatment. The journey was something like three or four hundred miles, and for a sick man an exceedingly tiring affair, but he arrived there safely.

After McGregor departed Williams and I travelled with the cattle to the junction of the Zambesi and Kafue, established a camp on the far side of the river, and had a Titan's task transporting the animals across. The river was fully seven hundred yards wide at the narrowest reaches, the water deep, and the current swift. In order to get the cattle over, two good paddlers jumped into a canoe, the beasts were forced into the river, and were caught one at a time and dragged into deep water. The mouth of each animal was secured on top of the dug-out, while another man held the beast by the tail and pulled him against the boat, sideways on; canoe and animal then floated across. On account of the force of the current some of the frightened beasts landed a thousand yards away from the intended point. After reaching the bank on the opposite side, the first thing we had to do was to look for a hippo path, to enable the boys to emerge from the tangled undergrowth of the banks. It was slow work, for it generally took two or three hours before the boys could land with an ox on the far side.

Everywhere the Zambesi teemed with crocodiles, and the crossing of the animals was therefore a noisy process, for we all yelled and shouted at the top of our voices to frighten the loathsome brutes. The natives never under-estimated the cunning of their hereditary enemy, and each village erected a landing-place by driving poles into the water and constructing a platform from which water was scooped. I once saw a woman captured by a crocodile on the Kafue while obtaining water. The whole thing happened in an instant. The crocodile does not kill its victim, but pulls it under the water and drowns it.

We made a pleasant camp for ourselves on the south bank

of the Zambesi, just at the junction of the Kafue and in direct line from the cattle kraals. Williams and I stayed here for some time, but did little hunting as we were expecting McGregor to return with more trading goods, and were constantly on the look-out for him. McGregor, however, was delayed, and Williams became very impatient, on account of the monotony, so that as soon as McGregor arrived he expressed a strong desire to proceed to Salisbury. Williams asked for his share of the cattle, which we gave him, and he then departed on his long trek to the south.

McGregor and I went once more into the Mashukulumbwe district, and traded more cattle. One afternoon we heard the bellowing of a lot of beasts in the bush, not far from us. We proceeded in the direction of the sound, and found an Indian, who was well educated and able to speak fluent English. It was always an event to come in contact with a stranger who was not a native, and we were pleased to meet one another. The Asiatic told us that his name was Naiker, and that he was a clerk to an Austrian, named Rabeneik. It seemed his beasts were dying like flies, and his boys informed me that on their way to the Kafue they had passed through a wide belt of tsetse fly, deadly to domesticated animals. We invited Naiker to our camp, and eventually decided to trek to the Zambesi together, but shortly after Naiker's arrival the natives became extremely hostile. At one particular village the chief had never exhibited friendly feelings, and we sensed trouble. Part of our daily routine was to shoot buck to supply the porters with meat, and one morning McGregor and Naiker went into the veld early. When midday came and they had not returned I wondered why they were so long away. I was lying in my tent when of a sudden I heard a tremendous commotion, war-cries, and a terrific din. I jumped up, grabbed my revolver from under my pillow, and in the entrance of my tent collided with the big chief himself. He was wearing a shell necklace, and as we met face to face I seized him by this and put my revolver in his face.

There were hundreds of warriors immediately behind him who rushed in with their assegais to spear me. I shouted to the chief that I would shoot him as soon as the first man attempted to kill me. They all knew that I meant what I said, and the chief called his men off; but they were so excited that they pushed and barged, and the chief and I were buffeted about like footballs. I managed, however, to keep my hold on him, using his body as a shield. My own natives fled into the bush. The struggle lasted for an appreciable time, and the chief kept on imploring me to let him go.

"I will," I told him, "if you make your men retire fifty yards, sit down, and not move. But at the first sign of treachery you die."

Next I heard a yell from the outer edge of the mob, and recognized the voices of McGregor and Naiker, who had been told that I was dead. They shouted, asking whether they should shoot. "No," I yelled, for that would have caused a battle. We could have shot a few of the savages, but certain death would have followed; they were hundreds to one. Our only security was my revolver pressed between the chief's eyes.

Eventually, with his support, I got the men to listen and retire, leaving the chief and myself together. I asked him why he wanted to kill me, and he replied that one of my boys had entered a hut in the village to buy wood from a woman who refused to sell. The boy then seized a stick, which I afterwards ascertained was a piece about four feet long and three inches thick. I asked the chief whether he would not settle this affair in some peaceful manner, and he then spoke with his counsellors, who agreed that a fine of five blankets be paid to the chief, and the boy who stole the wood should be punished. It was sheer, unadulterated blackmail, but, in such hazardous

69

circumstances, I paid up. The natives, however, refused to allow Naiker and McGregor to proceed northward, and after delivering this ultimatum, seized their spears and retired to their villages.

We bought Naiker's cattle, and made our way down to the Zambesi. McGregor soon decided that he had seen enough of the wilds for a time, and accordingly wended his way back to Salisbury. At that time cattle were quarantined in Southern Rhodesia, and we were not able to take the cattle over the border, so McGregor said he would select a white man on his arrival in Salisbury, and send him back to assist me in looking after the beasts; for I had declared that I was not remaining anchored to the camp, and intended going farther north.

It took several weeks for McGregor's man to reach me. He was about my age, named Kruis, very keen on hunting, and especially anxious to shoot a lion. Alas, he was fated never to get one.

One evening I took Kruis to a pool where I knew lions and rhinos came to drink. We sat there until ten o'clock, but could not stay longer because the mosquitoes were unbearable. As we rose to return to camp we heard a noise in the grass, and, looking towards the sound, I could just see a black object. I fired, and a form fell to the ground; it was a water-buck, which we left for the boys to collect next morning. At daybreak we took our rifles and a few boys, went to the spot where I had shot the buck, and told the natives to take it back to camp. We looked round for more buck but saw none, and decided to separate and hunt along different lines of country. It was agreed that Kruis should go to the top of the bank of the river, on the off-chance of securing an antelope, and I should hunt for hippo on the sand-bank.

Late in the afternoon a native commenced shouting from the far bank. He was a considerable distance away; the shouts of the natives working on the hippo were deafening, and it was difficult to hear what he was saying. The message, however, sounded as if a white man had been killed by lions. I immediately rushed into a dug-out and paddled across to the boy, who informed me that he had been out to obtain honey and roots from the bush when he heard near-by screams. A little way off he found a white man lying on the ground and unable to move, while marks on the earth showed that the "Mezungu" had been attacked by lions. The native led us to the spot, and there I found poor Kruis, badly mauled, still conscious, and in dreadful agony.

In faltering words, punctuated by gasps, he explained that shortly after leaving me he had come upon four lions lying in the open. He fired and wounded one, and the others went off, the injured one following. He traced the blood spoor, but he had gone only thirty yards when another lion leapt out from behind an ant-hill, jumped right on top of him, and knocked his rifle out of his hand. The lion attacked his legs. At the time Kruis was wearing a fine pair of Bedford cord riding-breeches, which were now in rags, and just above the knee the flesh looked like mince-meat, while all the muscles had been torn. After this, Kruis said, the lion just went off and he rolled over to get his rifle. The beast, however, happened to look round, and, seeing that his victim was still alive, came back. Kruis got hold of the lion's mouth with two hands, and the fingers of the right hand were practically severed. He then lay perfectly still, and the lion departed into the dense bush. It was lucky that the native had been looking for the honey and roots, otherwise Kruis might never have been found.

He was quite unable to move, and the boys and I made a stretcher from the branches of trees and carried him back to camp, where I bandaged and bathed his wounds. All night long he was delirious, and kept calling for his father. It was hopeless from the first; the shock had been too great. Throughout the night the lions came back on our spoor, and roared continually outside our rondavels. Kruis would not allow me to go out and shoot; in fact, he would not let me leave his side. The next day I made up my mind to follow them. I tracked them for a thousand yards from the camp, and then I noticed a lion leap through the bush. I just got a glimpse of him and ran in his direction, when I came right on top of an elephant bull. The moment I raised my rifle I saw that the animal was on his knees, with his hind legs almost upright. I walked up to him and saw that he was dead, and that the lions had torn open the stomach; they had been feeding on him for two days. On examination I found that it was an elephant that I had shot three days previously when a herd had walked through my camp. I had fired, and they had cleared away; seeing no signs of blood, I had come to the conclusion that the spoor was not worth while trailing.

I returned to the camp after this to see how Kruis was progressing, and told him of the elephant. He said he would like to see the tusks — which weighed sixty pounds each. Then I left again to find the lions. With two boys we took up the spoor, and, about three hundred yards away from the ant-hill where we had found Kruis, we saw that the beasts had gone into the dense bush. I took my shot-gun, which I always preferred to any other weapon for close-range work with carnivorous soft-skinned animals. Just about ten yards inside the bush a lion emitted a deafening roar and charged us. I waited until he was three or four paces away, and fired. He dropped at once.

When I returned to camp poor Kruis was *in extremis*. From then on he mercifully became unconscious, and on the evening of the third day he died. I buried him under a large baobab-tree, near the banks of the Zambesi.

In contests with wild beasts victory does not always go to the man with the gun. Another occasion comes to mind when a buffalo, plunging and fighting in the bush, left a trail of disaster, nonchalantly tossing my boys from his path, and knocking me down.

We were on our way from Portuguese territory, whither we had travelled for supplies, when, passing a small island, I heard a woman calling. She said there was a big buffalo on the island. We landed and made camp. It was not much of a place to hide such a large animal, being some thousand by four hundred yards, but it was very thickly covered with bush, and the undergrowth was a mass of brambles, with high reeds near the river. Elephants and buffaloes will cross wide stretches of water just for a change of diet, and on this island the msowa-tree grew with its tempting fruit, which is almost the size of a cherry, yellow, and tasting rather like an apple. The woman led me straight to the spoor, which was certainly that of a big buffalo bull that had crossed during the night from the west bank on the mainland, attracted by the sweet smell of the msowa fruit.

It was then rather late in the afternoon, but I followed the trail in order to ascertain whether the buffalo was still on the island, and soon came upon a hippo path where the under-growth had been trodden bare, the high, thick reeds on either side leaning to meet above, forming a veritable tunnel. The buffalo tracks had gone down this tunnel. While I was stand-ing regarding them, my only companion a dog, and coming to the conclusion that it would be wise to wait for the good light of morning before taking up the hunt, a grunt quite close in the reeds told me the quarry had spotted me, and had himself turned hunter. He was approaching; and suddenly he appeared a mere pace or two in front of me, his head down near the ground, threatening. It happened with such startling abruptness that my instinctive shot was unsuccessful, and I jumped to evade the beast. The buffalo made not for me but for my dog, goring him and tossing him aside. Then he broke into the reeds, and I was left with my little comrade dead. I swore vengeance for him.

The woman told me that among the natives across the river there were some good hunters, so I sent a message and invited them to join me. Next morning ten natives, armed with spears and bows-and-arrows, arrived. It was the first adventure of the kind I had ever taken part in with natives. We crept on hands and knees into the awful brambly undergrowth for about five hundred yards, when the buffalo indicated his presence by loud grunts. He did not charge, but broke away into the bush. We followed him nearly across the island, and I began to think that perhaps he had swum the river to the mainland, when, suddenly, the great bull charged me from the flank. He had changed his direction entirely, and had been lying in ambush waiting for us.

I was in a crouching position in the bush and could not see my target, for the beast had torn his way through the bush, and his horns and head were covered with foliage and leaves, which camouflaged him. I fired without effect, and as I got in my second shot the buffalo knocked me down. Fortunately for me, the bush covered his horns and I was not badly hurt, but I fell on my back with my rifle pointing upward, and the buffalo pinned me to the ground. I fired again at random, and the shot went into his neck, severing a main artery as I discovered later. He then left me alone, and made off along his original path. The natives were all running along this track, and the first boy he encountered, was knocked down. He happened to be my gun-bearer, and fortunately was not impaled, but when he scrambled up I saw that he appeared to be completely bewildered, and was holding the rifle the wrong way round with the stock in front.

"Bass, did you see him?" he shouted.

All the natives in the path of the buffalo were tossed, and everywhere grunts and shouts resounded. It was marvellous that not one man was killed, and only one badly injured. In his case one of the buffalo's horns had penetrated the upper arm, exposing and tearing the muscle badly. I followed the beast, which plunged into the river still bleeding copiously from the wound I had inflicted. I jumped into a canoe, continuing the pursuit, and on the other bank, after having gone a short distance, I found him dead.

Marauding beasts were a constant anxiety, not so much to our safety as to that of the cattle. There was one night when, knowing that lions were in the vicinity, the boys had erected a particularly strong scherm, or stockade, composed of thorn-trees. I had seen the spoor of the big cats, and, in case of attack, did not pitch my tent, but put up a stretcher just inside the entrance to the stockade, the "gate" being vicious-looking thorn-bushes. We kept a big fire burning.

It was in the middle of the night, after a half-moon had set, when I heard the snapping of twigs; the ominous, dull sound of a big animal landing from a leap; the piteous squeal of an animal in pain. Fright quickly spreads through a herd, and the cattle stampeded. Some of them collided with my stretcher, knocking it, and me, to the ground, and, leaping over, they broke through the stockade, heedless of thorn-lacerated skins.

In the rush I had lost my rifle, and I could do nothing to stop the maddened beasts as they leapt and crowded and raced off into the night. It was pretty dark, and what I did not know was that behind the stragglers of the herd was a lion. I thought the shape was just another of the cattle, and shouted in the hope of stopping it. A mighty roar answered, and I knew well enough then that it was a lion that leapt past me after the thundering herd. I heard a gurgling sound close to where I stood, holding at the ready my recovered rifle. It sounded like the choking of an ox, and two shapes were head to head not half a dozen paces from me. I could make out enough to realize that a lion had seized the ox by its muzzle. It was close enough for me, at a step forward, to be able to press the rifle against the lion. I pulled the trigger and the big cat's head was nearly blown off, while the injured ox ran into the bush, bellowing frantically.

There were lions still among the goats, and I used up some ammunition blindly, hoping to frighten them off. They were eventually scared by the din of our shouts and shots — or satisfied with their kill — for they disappeared, leaving us the difficult job of rounding up the cattle, which occupied us well into the morning. The raiders had not only injured several cattle, but got eight of my goats that night. May I add they got my goat too!

CHAPTER SIX

Lost Men of the Lost Lands

For a period I made my headquarters at a most appealing spot, at the confluence of the Zambesi and one of its two main tributaries — the Kafue. It was wild territory, haunted by the ghosts of early conquistadores and the romantic workers who, under Portuguese taskmasters, delved for silver at the lost mines of Chicova, which later many prospectors endeavored to rediscover.

This country offered adventure to my heart's desire, and exploration enticed me even more than big-game hunting. Beyond the Zambesi one large range of mountains stretched for hundreds of miles. The sierra was impassable, but here and there were monkey and native paths which led to nowhere. There were mountains on the eastern side of the river as well as on the western side, and here the rare white rhino roamed, while in the valley below there was an abundance of game, including elephant, buffalo, and black rhino.

The heat in the valley of dense undergrowth and bush was intense, and, away from the river, the country was waterless during the dry season. Insects which resembled flying crickets abounded. They were everywhere, and all day kept up a maddening noise like the continued ringing of a telephone.

Another "gogga" of the valley was a small insect, rather like a diminutive bee, known in Afrikaans as the "Moka" bee, in size smaller than the common house-fly, black in color, and devoid of any sting. These pests were in myriads, and got into my eyes, ears, nose, mouth, and hair, causing extreme discomfort — sometimes, indeed, agony. There were hundreds of their nests in the trees, and all contained small quantities of

77

honey, of which the natives were very fond, eating the comb as well as the young bees hatching out in the hive. I found the substance had a delicious flavor, much nicer than ordinary honey, and very satisfying.

I doubt if I have conjured up a real picture of the country in which I had established myself. Unclimbable mountains; forest and bush absolutely impenetrable, except along those paths the animals and the aborigines had made through the centuries; the singing currents of the big rivers; crocodiles on the mud; an occasional canoe shooting by, a monotonous dirge sung by the occupants. Hundreds of square miles to hunt over, the sniff of danger in the very air when one entered new territory where hostile tribes lived. The fascination of study-ing the animals, the birds, and, most of all, the inhabitants — remembering they were brother humans, with minds groping for knowledge buried in quaint superstitions, through which a glint of light penetrated now and then — all very much, per-haps, as some ancestors of our own lived thousands of years ago. Here, indeed, was escape from the "madding crowd" of far-off towns. It suited me.

I was intrigued — and not surprised — to learn, up there on the Zambesi, that there were other white men who had thrown off the cloak of civilization and had "gone native." One had read stories of such men; I was now to see two of them for myself. The natives told me of "a strange white man," who was a chief, a few days' journey from my camp, and I determined to seek him out. Following their directions, I came to a large, well-stockaded village near the river-bank. To the first natives encountered I explained my peaceful mission and without trouble, was brought into the presence of the chief.

He was a pukka white man all right.

It is not for me to reveal his identity, even at this date; and I was careful not to pry into his history — not that I thought there was anything shady about it. He had just wandered, much as I had done, tasting the heady wine of strange experiences off the beaten track, had become stranded, made friends with the natives, and stayed — the line of least resistance. By mere reason of his mental superiority it was inevitable that they should make him their chief, and there he had been for years, absolute ruler of two thousand souls.

"And you are satisfied? You never crave to return to your own kind?" I ventured.

Seated before me in loin-cloth and skin, blue eyes smiling from under bushy brows, teeth gleaming between heavy brown moustaches and beard, was no wastrel who had been compelled to fly the haunts of civilization, nor yet a bully who gloried lustfully in the power he held. He was a cultured man who had obviously once trodden no mean ways.

"I am satisfied," he replied in English.

He looked through the door of his hut into the clearing where his subjects passed, glancing inquisitively our way; he smiled as one of his two native wives — a comely wench of twenty, proud of her position and her gay print dress— brought in beer for our refreshment.

"What else does a man want?" he asked.

From time to time he even grew enthusiastic on the subject of the peace and pleasure of his days. His subjects provided everything he needed.

"Isn't it good enough for you?" he queried once. "Stay. We should be company for each other."

But I was not cut out for lotus-eating, and, though I enjoyed the week I stayed in his village, I then moved on. It was an item of information he let drop during our many talks that directed my course. This news was none other than that there was another white man living with natives some four days' journey away. He was a different type to my host, being a Portuguese and an outlaw. This man, Pedro, was "wanted" by the Rhodesian Government for store-breaking in Umtali, and had escaped into Portuguese territory, reaching that ancient post, Zumbo, on the British and Portuguese borders. He then proceeded to ingratiate himself with the big chief of the Chikunda tribe — the Paramount Chief Kanyemba — who, although living within seven miles of Zumbo, had never been conquered. He promised his protection to the fugitive, and gave him his eldest daughter in marriage.

Kanyemba was a powerful man who, like Mburuma, had other blood than Bantu in him; indeed, he looked very much like a Cape colored man, and was always expensively dressed in silk loin-cloths. Some little time before my arrival in the country the Portuguese authorities dispatched a patrol to arrest Pedro, but the outlaw shot and killed some of their askaris, and was then outlawed from Portuguese as well as British territory. He escaped along the Zambesi with his wife and some slaves given him by Kanyemba, and established himself at the junction of the Kafue and Zambesi, which was then no-man's land. He still had the protection of Kanyemba, who threatened to make war on any tribe offering resistance to Pedro, and, since the whole countryside went in fear of this chief, Pedro was left unmolested.

My host warned me if I went to Pedro's village I should be wise to proceed cautiously, as the desperado would almost certainly shoot on sight at a stranger; but if I could make friends he would be able to give me assistance in getting through the mountains to the lands beyond, and would supply me with guides and porters.

I decided to visit Pedro, but soon after commencing my journey I was stricken by a really bad bout of fever. I managed to reach a native village, where for two days I lay unconscious. As soon as I was able to take food my cook-boy brought me chicken broth, and I resolved to travel by canoe while the porters with their loads proceeded along the river-bank, keeping the canoe in sight.

Lost Men of the Lost Lands

The Zambesi was now in full spate, and had overflowed its banks into the bush. A rough bed was arranged for me in the bottom of the dug-out. As we were paddling along I heard an ominous grating noise just below me, sounding as if we had struck a rock or some other obstruction. To my consternation a hippo suddenly appeared at my side, and seizing the canoe in its powerful jaws, lifted it clean out of the water. The frail craft capsized, and I was thrown into the river, but luckily we were not far from the bank, for we were going upstream, which made it necessary to pole and therefore keep to the shallows. There were a number of trees floating downstream, and the boys helped me to seize one of these.

We now discovered the reason for the attack. The hippo had a small calf resting on one of the trees among an accumulation of branches and reeds. When the dug-out was righted I found that all our possessions were intact, for, knowing the danger of hippos in these rivers, the natives had tied all the impedimenta to the canoe with ropes.

I went ashore to dry my clothing, and the next day, though very weak, I set off again. When we reached the junction of the two rivers the natives warned me that I must keep out of sight and take the Portuguese outlaw by surprise, otherwise I should most certainly be killed. For a distance of four miles from Pedro's lair we therefore proceeded warily through the bush, and arrived at the village fairly late in the afternoon. Pedro had a large establishment, enclosed with reeds eight feet high, and, on nearing the gates, I saw the outlaw sitting inside with numerous women and men, all gathered round a pot of beer. He was attired only in a loin-cloth, and the moment he saw me fled into the hut in evident alarm, while the natives scattered in all directions. I called out to them in Mkorokora that I came as a friend, and was travelling through the country bent on peaceful trading. Pedro remained in the hut shouting excuses, but in ten minutes appeared, arrayed in a khaki shirt and trousers. Thereupon he shook hands, and I was invited inside. He pointed out a large new rondavel, which he placed at my disposal in order to dispense with tents. The rondavel was lined with native mats, and was clean and comfortable. Pedro went to much trouble to entertain me, giving me an excellent meal of chicken, pumpkin, and mealie meal, and also treated me with native herbs for fever. As the crowning act of generosity, when, that night, I proceeded to my rondavel, two young native-girls were offered for my entertainment! I stayed here for nearly a month, for I was very weak from malaria, and my porters were also down with fever. During my sojourn with Pedro I lived well. No wonder men such as he, who have gone native, are satisfied with their lot.

When I left Pedro told me that after three days' journey towards the west I would come to a vast plateau — later on, I found that the country he referred to was the Kafue flats. He supplied me with porters, so we set out again, and crossed the range of mountains to the north-west of the Zambesi — a journey which occupied two days, for the heat was intense and the climbing difficult. He warned me of a hostile tribe — the Mashukulumbwe — behind these mountains, living in open country, a savage people who did not permit a white man to cross their country. Thus I was not surprised when, on the fourth morning, I turned out to see a deputation of strange natives who had been sent from the big chief of the Mashukulumbwe tribe to instruct me not to proceed any farther into their land. They added that their chief would inspect me the next day.

In the morning several warriors, each of whom appeared to be seven feet high, approached the camp. They advanced in extended order with their assegais thrust forward, and soon I found myself standing with a dozen of these unpleasant weapons pressed against my chest, while the leader of the party uttered a native greeting which meant, "Good morning, my friend." The way he said it was grim and ominous, and I admit to having felt decidedly uncomfortable, especially when I remembered Pedro's warning. However, seeing I made no show of fight, the assegais were withdrawn, though obviously held at the "ready," and I was ordered by the chief to accompany him to the tribal god in the mountains. If the god agreed to my continuing my journey, he said, no further objections would be raised; if not, I must return. There was nothing for it but to go with the savages — I was in no position to argue.

We marched for ten miles towards the north, until we reached some big rapids in the Kafue river, and beyond the cascades clustered the huts of a village. I was now commanded to sit down outside while the Mashukulumbwe held an indaba. After a while they returned to me where I squatted, and I was informed that I would be taken to the place of their god. We set off for this Negro heaven to ascertain the edict of this pagan deity. It was a strange and somewhat alarming excursion and mystical pilgrimage, headed by the chief, myself following him, and behind us an escort of one hundred tall warriors, whose skin shone like greased ebony in the stinging sunshine.

After a lengthy tramp we reached a high, overhanging cliff, below which the ground had reverently been swept. When we had proceeded half-way along the cliff face the chief called for silence, and presently I noticed two huge tusks of ivory lying at the far end of the cliff. Here too were hippo skeletons, and I was signalled to a hippo's skull as a seat, while the chief approached the tusks. With his head bowed low, praying and clapping his hands, he beseeched the god for fully half an hour. He then returned, and said that the deity consented to my continuing my journey provided I continued to shoot, but he warned me that I must not do any shooting on that hallowed day.

I regarded the whole ceremony as an absurd ritualistic mumbo-jumbo which would provide meat, and observing that twenty yards from us there were at least two dozen hippo in the water, I asked the chief's permission to shoot one for the pot.

"Fire if you like, but you will not kill," that despot replied. Curiously enough, although I fired several shots, I did not kill a single hippo that day — why I do not know; was it tagati — black magic?

So I entered into the land of the Wa-ila, or Mashuku-lumbwe, a strange and warlike tribe possessing vast herds of cattle, who had chased Selous and Dr. Holub, the Austrian explorer, out of the country.

The adults of the tribe had no front teeth in the top jaw, for on reaching the age of sixteen their molars were extracted. I often witnessed extractions, which were regarded as an initiation ceremony, proclaiming the victims to have come of age. The medicine man was in attendance, and those who were to undergo the operation took their places in rows, all squatting on their haunches. The medicine man then proceeded to perform his barbaric rites. Each victim in turn rested elbows on knees with the chin on the open palms of the hands. The dentist's implement was an ordinary native axe made from a piece of crude iron, six inches long and a quarter of an inch thick, but tapering to a fine point. The thin end of the iron was inserted into a handle made from particularly strong wood, and in this a hole was burnt to hold the axe — which was used as a chisel, and was placed against the tooth, the handle being removed from the axe at this particular stage. Another axe was employed as a hammer, and the medicine man proceeded to knock first on the right side of the jaw, and then on the left, until the teeth were sufficiently loosened to be removed with the fingers. Meanwhile a pot of water in which herbs had been boiled was produced, and this fluid was used to rinse the bleeding mouth. This singularly painful process was then considered to be completed, and the patients had the satisfaction of knowing that they had attained to manhood's estate. The Mashukulumbwe regard with contempt any native exhibiting upper teeth, and would never marry into a tribe the members of which possessed normal molars.

Their Paramount Chief was called Maunsi, and he had numerous other important indunas under him.

One of these villages, named after Chief Mninga, afterwards became a regular camping place of mine. Mninga had seven wives, the eldest of whom supervised the preparation of my food. When the meal was ground it would be placed in baskets, and the chief's wife would walk at the head of a row of women, each carrying on her head a load of food which would be exchanged for beads, or, if there was a large quantity, for calico. The men of the tribe were practically nude, but the women were quite well dressed, wearing the skin of the Puku antelope, reaching from the waist downward — the upper portion of the body was never clothed.

I became quite friendly with the eldest wife of Mninga, who always warned me against any secret plotting which might endanger me. These people had their own laws, and in cases of murder from poisoning or other cause they demanded a life for a life and an eye for an eye. The subjects of the Paramount Chief were not allowed to take the law into their own hands, and the punishment for a murder fully fitted the crime, since the accused was led out of the village and beaten to death with kerries (clubs).

On one occasion, when I was camping at Mninga's village, the eldest wife sent a messenger to me, saying that her husband was very ill and was about to die. The alarming message continued that she too had to die the next day because she had been accused of placing poison in the chief's food, and she asked me whether I could save her. Immediately

I went to see what had happened, and found that the medicine man had accused her by throwing the bones. Now, all you may have read about medicine men in native tribes is probably true. They have absolute power, and there is no appeal against their judgments. This dark lady friend of mine seemed doomed, but I was determined to do all I could to save her, for I was sure she was entirely innocent of this crime.

Mninga had been carried outside the hut into the sun, and was lying on an old ox-skin. He appeared to be desperately ill, so I sat down next to him and asked him to open his mouth, for I suspected malaria. His tongue was absolutely yellow. He looked pitifully at me.

"I can cure you," I told him, "but I will do it on one condition. You have accused your wife of having poisoned you, and I understand she is to be killed to-morrow. Is that true?" To which he replied, "That is quite true."

"That death sentence on your wife must be cancelled, then I will cure you," I said.

Very quickly he called his indunas together, told them what I had said — and they agreed to my terms. I commenced to treat the chief with purgatives and large doses of quinine, and remained with him for two weeks until he was cured. True to his promise, the wife was spared her life.

CHAPTER SEVEN

Death in the Jungle

LIFE IS HELD cheaply in Zambesia. Feuds, punishments, barbaric rites, tribal wars, cannibalism, slave raids — all take constant toll of the population. Within my own experience there was at least one deliberate, cold-blooded murder, done so that a son might step into his inheritance. That particular crime of the jungle had difficult repercussions for me, sending me a fugitive into the wilds under sentence of death.

It was altogether a queer business. I had gone to a village, hitherto unvisited, where lived a Paramount Chief, named Chyawa, who held undisputed sway over an area extending fully a hundred miles to the west of the river. Having made contact with his men, I was told to await him under a certain tree. Meeting a tribe or a chief for the first time always held an element of excitement. He might greet one with the native gusto of seizing one's hand in both of his, or he might bring a hundred braves to point a hundred assegais at one's chest. Chyawa was unique; he did neither. He came to me hesitant and nervous as a lad stepping out of class for reprimand — and this in spite of his distinguished appearance. He was tall, commanding, though slender, white-haired, possibly seventy years of age, wearing a kaross of wild-cat skin that fell from his shoulders almost to his feet.

It turned out subsequently that he was in this somewhat disturbed state of mind because I was the first white man he had ever seen. What was troubling him was revealed in his first remark.

"I have lived so long," he said gravely, "and now you have come to kill me."

It did not take long to persuade him that I had other ideas; that all I wanted of him was his help to get me forward towards the Congo, whither I was bound. Relieved, he promised me all the porters I needed, and we had a friendly indaba, in which I endeavored to satisfy his childish curiosity about the country and the ways of the pale-faces.

My camp was pitched on the other side of the river, for it is well to arrange friendly relations ahead when possible, and when we parted I returned, stayed a night, and then got my supplies across to the waiting carriers. Early in the morning I was off, for we had a long trek ahead of us — a hundred and sixty miles up the Zambesi to reach the foot of a high mountain, known as Kabira, where, we were told, we should strike a baboon path into the Bassouri country.

That was the last I ever saw of Chyawa.

The first night out we pitched camp at the junction of the Zambesi and a tributary called the Luangwa, where the river ran deep and the jungle closed in like a wall. From the thicket came, with nightfall, the roar of lions, but after we had lit fires and set pickets the camp slept peacefully. It was just a typical jungle night, and my rest would have been undisturbed until daybreak had I not been roused by one of the boys, who asking for admission, came in to say that a woman urgently desired to see me. Rather mystified, I bade her enter. She was no longer young, and her eyes were dull with pain. Her two hands were clasped, and when she spoke her voice held that note of flat resignation typical of native fatalism.

"Where is Chyawa?" she asked.

"I have not seen him since we left the village," I told her, surprised at her question. "What has happened?"

"Chyawa is no longer there," she replied.

I pressed her for particulars, but could make little of the

rambling story she told, mostly in monosyllables, answering my cross-examination. I gathered that the chief's eldest son, Kanyemo by name, had visited the chief, in company with one of my boys whom we called Jonas. This boy had been left in charge of my camp to look after the cattle which were corralled there. These two young men had begged the chief to go with them to settle some marriage problem, and the last that had been seen of Chyawa was when he had walked off with the others along a track. Since Jonas was my boy she had come to make inquiries.

I thought the best thing to do was to send a head-man back to the village to investigate and bring me the facts, and he went off in company with the woman. I waited four days before the induna returned, though it was only one day's journey each way.

No doubt during that time members of the tribe had plotted with him, but of this, of course, I knew nothing. The induna indeed silenced my doubts — as was probably intended — for he stated definitely that Chyawa was in his village and Jonas was at my camp. Naturally it relieved me, and, putting the whole affair down to a woman's imagination, I forgot it and pushed on.

The trip was interesting. At one big chief's village — he rejoiced in the musical name of Chitendavunga — I ran into slave-traders up from Chukunda, who were exchanging muzzle-loaders, powder caps, and blankets for human serfs, and the chief himself exchanged presents with me. I was still blandly unaware that Chyawa had been murdered, and that I was under sentence of death.

It was here, however, I began to realize that something was wrong. My boys had gone off to a beer-drink, leaving me alone; and in the afternoon, going for a stroll — for the country had changed from jungle to open veld — I noticed in the distance hundreds of natives fully armed, their spears and assegais glittering in the sunlight. They were obviously on the war-path, and I did not betray my presence, but doubled back for camp. The boys returned, but I made up my mind to keep a careful watch, and, on the excuse of illness, had a big fire lighted and took my position near to it. The last thing I knew I must do was to exhibit any alarm.

Nothing happened, and we broke camp early, travelling through treeless country. After eight miles or so from a ridge we saw a large village; this belonged to Diempe, Chyawa's brother, and we made for it through a swampy valley. Then, again, I saw in impi — more natives on the war-path — and, now, not able to avoid them, I shouted a greeting. They disappeared, and we moved on to within a mile of the village. Here my boys halted, saying they were tired, and I strolled on, urged by a restlessness that the series of suspicious events doubtless occasioned.

Crisis came suddenly. Hundreds of natives sprang up behind me, and were obviously making for the camp. I could see I should be cut off, and shouted to one of my boys to bring me revolver and rifle. My personal servant answered, running to me with my rifle, and I stood there and saw the natives enter camp — to be welcomed by Chyawa's men, who calmly handed over all their loads! Having possessed themselves of everything, the warriors turned towards me. It looked a pretty hopeless proposition to put up a show against so many; there was however, a kopje at hand, and I clambered to the top of it. My boy ran off in fear, while the natives completely surrounded the mound.

"I shoot the first man who attempts to ascend," I yelled at them, but the threat was unheeded by several, who commenced to assail my stronghold. I had to fire at their feet to persuade them discretion was the wiser course. It held them, causing them to gather and argue; in the end they made off for the village. I was left alone in my glory — a cold glory, for it was freezing. I had nothing on but khaki shirt and trousers, and I dared not leave my vantage point to cogitate upon what had caused the natives to rise against me! It was to be several days before I knew.

The first glimmer of daylight saw me on the move — back towards the Zambesi, living as I went on wild figs and honey. Once I thought the natives had followed me, for stones were obviously being rolled down the mountain-side towards where I chanced to be resting for a few minutes. Jumping up, I held my rifle at the ready, but no impi appeared; instead, three men came out of the bush, and one man at once spoke my name — "Mtanda Bantu."

When he approached near there was no need for him to tell me who he was. I recognized him as Chyawa's second son. He asked me, naturally enough as I thought, where was my safari, and I replied evasively that they were returning by another route, since I wanted to explore the mountains.

"You cannot go that way," he asserted. "Unscalable cliffs and precipices prevent," and he gestured to indicate the enormity of those impossible ups and downs. "But," he added, "yonder lies a native footpath, and in two days' time you will arrive at a village." He said he would come along and show me, explaining that he was returning there from a visit to relations. I agreed; it would have raised his suspicions had I refused. Moreover, I was alone, and not at all sure where I was.

We camped together that night, making a stockade and lighting fires. Once in the darkness I was disturbed by stealthy noises, and was on the alert, but soon knew the noises were made not by humans but by prowling lions. To an ear accustomed to the sounds of the wilds it is easy to detect a cat stalking prey — one step at a time, pausing between each to listen, rustling the grass as it moves again; which is in striking contrast to the hyena, trotting as it does at a slow pace, or of a leopard, which is never heard at all until it is almost on top of one.

But relief was short-lived. We approached the village next day, and I was assured I would be quite safe, since it was occupied by relations of Chyawa's. There was a stream to cross, and the moment we reached the other side and were visible to the inhabitants they all, as at a prearranged signal, plunged into their huts and came racing out, brandishing weapons.

"What's it mean?" I asked my companion.

"My father sleeps; you also must sleep," was his ominous answer.

I had a flashing impression that I had been the victim of a plot — though even then I did not realize the motive behind it — and had been artfully led into this very real danger. It was a moment for quick action, and, probably because Chyawa's son felt I was securely trapped, he was not ready for my jump. I was across that stream before he grasped the fact that I had moved, and had plunged into the bush. The natives yelled and beat their drums, but I evaded their tracks, doubled about on my course, and had the intense relief of hearing their noises grow distant. I was headed up a mountain-side, to climb which I had to ease myself forward from one tree-trunk to another. No one followed, and I pressed on — racked by thirst and hunger — until night came down, finding me wandering a little aimlessly in densely wooded kloofs. It was the gruff bark of baboons that led me to water, and I drank my fill — though I wish I had waited until daylight beside the pool to see its condition!

Still, the day brought me one welcome sight — that of the Zambesi away in the distance. It gave me hope; it gave me direction, and I covered sixteen miles of particularly hard-going before, late in the afternoon, I reached the Kafue, and knew the way to Pedro's place. I met a native here who told me Pedro was in camp, and that my boy who had brought the rifle to me near Diempe's village had arrived there, saying I had been killed. This native, whom I knew, paddled me across the river. Here I was met with a very different story. Pedro's wives informed me that my boy had never been there, and that Pedro himself had gone away! Some one was lying — and I didn't think it was my native friend.

I now began to fear foul play, for I conjectured that they were keeping my boy, and that the Portuguese was probably in hiding.

I had a hunch not to stay in the village; so I pushed on, and it chanced that I nearly collided with a native who was friendly towards me. He greeted me with the question that was now becoming familiar: "Why are you not killed?" This "boy," I might mention, was the tallest native I have ever seen in any part of Africa, being well over seven feet high. I told him that I knew nothing of what had been happening, and then at length I heard the truth.

The Paramount Chief Chyawa had been murdered. And where I came into the picture was that one of the murderers was the boy Jonas, whom I had left in charge of my camp.

It appeared that the eldest son of the chief had asked Jonas to help in the murder of his father, who, he said, was too old to rule. The son wanted to be Paramount Chief. He had offered one of his sisters to Jonas, and had also promised to make him a head-man. Jonas agreed; the two went to the old chief, and on the excuse that they wanted him to settle some marriage problem, conducted him into the woods.

I had left a little pet monkey in my boy's care, and Jonas had this animal with him, attached to a long chain. That chain became the means of execution. He would it suddenly round the unsuspecting Chyawa's neck, and, pulling it tight, calmly strangled the old man. The outrage was soon discovered, and, instead of becoming chief, the tribe made the son an outcast —

a pretty dreadful punishment in the jungle-lands — and ordered that Jonas should be roasted alive. And as I was Jonas's master I too had to die. That explained all that had happened. In their own peculiar way they had been sleuthing me, leading me to captivity, the second son—who had been proclaimed Paramount Chief — taking the part of chief tracker.

My friend, the tall native, rounded off his story with the information that there was another white man in the neighborhood. It was always an event to meet one of these rare traders, for at that time there might not be a civilized person over thousands of miles of territory. I made up my mind to visit the stranger, and found him a rather dishevelled person, with tremendous moustaches and a potential beard. His name was Williams, and, after shaking hands and discovering who I was, he proceeded to rate me roundly, his reason being that, as I had killed Chyawa, I had put an end to trade in the Zambesi, and he was about to return, disgusted, to Salisbury. A few sparks flew before he was made to understand that I was innocent, and then he told me that a Captain Hall and Mr. Taberer, the Chief Native Commissioner, were at my camp opposite Chyawa's village. No such officials had ever been so far north before, but I was glad of their presence and soon went to find them.

They were at my place all right — though on the point of departure. And they had Jonas with them, having rescued the boy from the natives, "though," pointed out Taberer, "I had no right to, because all this country is really no-man's land." I didn't recognize Jonas; he was completely changed after all he had gone through. He had been placed on a raised platform, and the outraged residents of the village had come along whenever they felt like it and thrown a bundle of lighted grass under him. His back was a ghastly sight, roasted and raw. He had certainly asked for trouble, but the sight of the form it had taken was nauseating.

94

Death in the Jungle

We talked over his case and agreed that he would have to be punished, since my life was forfeit as long as he lived, and Taberer suggested I should take him into Portuguese territory, since he was a Portuguese subject. This I did, and returning to my old position at the junction of the Kafue and Zambesi, close to Pedro's village, I interviewed the surrounding chiefs, informed them that I had nothing to do with Chyawa's murder, and that Jonas had been punished. They called an indaba, and agreed to leave me in peace.

And so, on the old friendly footing with my immediate neighbors, I continued my life as huntsman and trader for the remainder of my three years' stay in those parts. When at last I moved it was not in the hope of finding better hunting country; I doubt if such existed. The territory simply teemed with game of all descriptions. During the whole of my wanderings in Africa I never saw such a variety or such quantities of our fauna as I observed there — great troops of zebra, and hundreds of antelopes of different species, all feeding together, with lions lying quite close to the grazing animals.

It is a remarkable fact that when a lion has eaten his kill he ignores the buck and zebras, who instinctively do not fear him, and continue their feeding. But when a pride of hungry lions is lying in the vicinity of the antelopes, all the members of the herd keep their eyes on the carnivores. In the Kafue flats I often watched the maneuvers of lions and antelopes. Immediately the lion charges, the bucks stampede, sometimes only retreating a few yards. When they are aware that the lions have caught one of their companions the other animals then become quiet and continue feeding as if no tragedy had taken place.

It was here that I came across large packs of African hunting dogs — commonly known as wild dogs. I myself think that this term is a misnomer, as the African hunting dog is a species

entirely of its own. Its spoor alone is sufficient to distinguish it
from any of the canine race.

In size the wild dog fits in between the hyena and jackal, and
in height it ranges from two to two and a half feet, with a slight
easing off towards the hindquarters. He is mostly dark-grey in
color, but bears curious mottled splotches of white and yellow
on his coat, and has a white tip to the tail. His body is of the
same build as the jackal, but the ears are distinctly different,
being much larger, and rounded instead of pointed.

There were hundreds of wild dogs here among the herds of
gazelle. They are nasty creatures as they do not kill outright.
When they give chase they run in regular formation, one
following the other at even distances. Immediately a wild dog
reaches a buck he bites, tears the flesh from the ribs or hindquarters, and eats it as he gallops along. The buck can never
outdistance the wild dog, and when it eventually drops the
poor animal has probably had its entrails torn out and eaten
during the chase.

These dogs do not attack simultaneously, and if they are
hunting in country where they lose sight of one another they
have a call, rather like a cooee, a sort of drawn-out "hoo." This
call from the leader is passed on from one dog to the other in
succession, and is a signal to the hindermost one to leave the
trail, and cut across to stop a pursued animal. During the night
one hears them pursuing their quarry, and every minute the
call is passed on. Once I was in my camp when I heard this call.
I could hear the dogs, and knew that they were coming on in a
crescent formation in my direction. A few yards away there
was a small ravine, and in a short time I heard their pleased
little yaps, just like ordinary dogs', and the thud of the buck
falling in the ravine. I have always disliked wild dogs intensely, and have endeavored to exterminate them to the best of my
ability. These animals are hated and loathed by all who come

A lion shot by the Author from the Saddle (see p. 99)

Photo A. B. Verbi

into contact with them, and the only thing I can say in their favor is that they are remarkable hunters.

Before leaving Zambesia I started to capture live game for African zoos. It was a most exciting sport. Game was plentiful, and I caught zebra, wildebeest, and eland with comparative ease. On my horse (probably the only one for hundreds of miles) I would approach within one hundred yards of the animal, and start chasing right away with the sole object of a speedy capture. And it must be a quick success or a failure, for an antelope will run for miles and miles, outstaying any horse.

Lichtenstein's hartebeest and the sassaby are impossible to capture on horseback, for they are the swiftest of the antelope. On my first attempt I pursued a hartebeest for a mile, and then found that I had set myself a hopeless task, for he kept fifty yards ahead the whole time. I then endeavored to run him down in short sharp rushes, but with equally futile results, for, swift as my horse was, it was impossible to catch up with him.

My method was to approach close to a herd, give chase, and at the same time hit out at the animals with a sjambok. They would then scatter, and I would lasso the animal that I wanted, throwing the lariat over the neck, and tying a knot to obviate the choking of the beast.

I would often capture as many as seven wildebeest in a forenoon. My custom was to leave camp early in the morning with six or seven of my best boys, who each carried a reim (which is a leather thong made from the hide of cattle or buck.) When I secured a captive I took a reim, tied it round the neck of the animal, and the boy was then sent off to camp leading it. I found that antelopes were not difficult to lead, with the exception of the roan antelope, which would struggle and bite and kick violently. It required three boys, at least, to lead a roan; even a small calf of about six months old would put up a most glorious fight to retain its freedom. The eland too could be dangerous, for he would kick and lash out his hind-

97

legs with terrific force, but, peculiarly enough, seldom used his horns. The zebra could fight, and, unless taken very young, required very careful handling.

On one occasion I handed over four zebras to my boys to take back to camp. I had my own reim, and decided to catch one more and take him back myself. I got near a well-grown animal, about eighteen months old, and, leaning from my horse while he was still galloping, threw my reim round its neck. I then maneuvered closer to the animal, intending to tie the knot in the reim. But the thong was suddenly pulled through my hands, and the zebra lashed out and kicked me in the jaw with his hind-leg. Some time later I regained my senses, feeling very dazed, and noticed that my clothing was smothered in blood. The whole of my chin was cut open right to the bone, which fortunately, however, was not broken. My horse was standing a few yards away grazing peacefully. I looked in all directions, and, although I could see for miles in this open country, there was not a trace of a zebra. They had all vanished, so I painfully mounted my horse and made my way back to camp, a sadder and wiser man.

During three months I captured sixty-four head of game, nearly all of the three varieties — wildebeest, zebra, and eland. One morning I went out with a few boys to catch some game, when I saw a herd of wildebeest close to some scattered clumps of bush. As I approached I observed that, although they had noticed me, their heads were all turned in the opposite direction. I knew at once that there must be lions near by, and, riding along quietly, sure enough, I saw a lion about fifty yards on the other side of the wildebeest, crouching behind a stump of a tree, with his head protruding, and watching the herd closely. I quickly took my rifle from my bearer, and approached. I then saw that, about eighty yards beyond him, there were three lionesses, and these suddenly betrayed alarm, beginning to move off, while the lion arose and followed them.

98

It was level country, and, thinking to test the speed of the lion, I gave chase. The lionesses raced off at a great speed, but the male was much slower and kept on looking behind and grunting.

Although I was about thirty yards behind, the lion would not exert himself to the utmost, and I made up my mind that if he turned I would not shoot, but make a retreat and let him chase me. And this actually happened, for, with one big grunt, he swung to attack, and chased me for about a quarter of a mile. I could not get away from him, although my horse was doing its utmost, so I came to the conclusion that a lion has a fine turn of speed, and can run down any animal with the exception of the members of the hartebeest family. As the lion was now too close to be comfortable, I turned and shot him from the saddle. Ten boys were needed to carry the carcase; we procured a pole and tied the legs together around the pole, and with five men on each end they were unable to travel for more than a hundred yards at a time, for that particular lion was enormously heavy.

The ordinary lion is not a man-eater by nature, and, unless provoked, it pretty harmless to humans. But there are man-eaters, and, while I condemn the theory that these are animals which have become too old to hunt their usual prey, some unusual circumstance has, in my experience, always contributed to the habit.

On one occasion I was in Portuguese Nyasaland, at a little village called Tungi Bay (which is near Cape Delgado), with a friend, Captain Hemming. We were well known in the district, for we hunted there over a period of five years. As we were arriving at our animal camp, we were met just outside the village by a bearer with a note from a Portuguese official, warning us not to pitch tents at our usual spot but to come to the village and stay there, as there were numerous man-eating lions in the vicinity. We sent back a word of thanks for the advice, but declared that we were not afraid and would prefer to make camp in the usual place, which we did.

Between the tents we set up a big tarpaulin, under which we had our meals. That evening the camp-fires were all burning, while about a hundred chattering natives were round them, only thirty yards from the tents. After we had finished our supper we left our boy to clear the table and went into my tent. The moment we entered we heard a terrified scream. I knew that a lion was on the war-path, so Hemming and I seized our rifles, and, as soon as we got outside the tent, a lion carrying a native in his jaws passed within ten yards of us. The unfortunate native was not dead, for he kept calling, "Help me, master! Help, help!" I ran at once, hoping to get a short-range shot so that I could hit the lion without harming the boy, but in the darkness this was hopeless. The lion for a moment dropped the man, and as he did so, bit him, and killed him outright. I followed the beast as best I could, and as I cautiously felt my way I could hear the body being dragged along the ground. Presently I reached thick bush, which at this point continued for a mile right up to the mountains. I got within three or four paces of the beast, when the lion again commenced dragging, eating as he went.

Hemming had gone back for a lantern, and on his return we continued into the bush for fully half a mile, when we found that the lion had completely finished the victim. We had to give up the chase, for the man-eater decamped into the darkness.

The next evening a lion caught a woman, about four miles away on top of a hill. We reached the spot as quickly as we could, but there was nothing of the woman left except a few small bones. The murderous raids continued for eight days, never two days passing without a new victim being claimed. Eventually we had a drive for the man-eater and cornered him near the sea, where we shot him. We then found that he had only three sound legs, one, apparently, having been broken years previously in a native trap. Handicapped in this manner, the lion was obviously not able to hunt game, and had therefore been compelled by hunger to become a confirmed man-eater.

In 1904 a native rebellion broke out in German East Africa, well organized by witch-doctors who quietly had been preparing the ground for more than a year. When everything was in readiness all the natives in the territory were to revolt, the signal for action being the rising of the new moon. At the stated time the natives advanced along the Rufiji river to a village named Nakarsiku, and a large company of German troops proceeded to intercept them. Within a day's march of this particular village there is a swamp between the river and a small lake, and the Germans had hidden in a cotton field on the east side of the swamp during the night. The next morning the natives attacked in mass formation, and advanced to within a hundred yards of the Germans, who opened fire with machine-guns and killed several hundreds of the insurgents.

The reeds along the Rufiji spread for two or three hundred yards, and constituted wonderful breeding places for lions. The lion often became a scavenger, and here on the Rufiji the beasts went after these dead bodies and dragged them to the reeds, where they had a surfeit of human flesh. As a result this district became one of the very worst places for man-eaters I have ever known.

Apart from human beings the most dangerous enemy of the lion is the porcupine, which is very much sought after by them as a delectable tit-bit. When he comes upon a porcupine he rushes the creature, and immediately the porcupine erects his quills for protection. The lion does not hesitate to squash his victim with his paw, killing it with one rapid death-stroke. As he strikes the porcupine his paw becomes full of quills which are covered with fine barbs. The lion chews off these quills as far as they protrude, but the barbs frequently penetrate into the flesh, and also, when biting off the quills, they get into the lion's mouth. This leads to inflammation, and poisoning sets in rapidly. I cannot say how long it takes, but I have often found lions in such a condition that the claws have dropped off. I have frequently observed lions not only without claws, but with the jaws and cheeks frightfully mutilated where the quills have penetrated, and the tongue so festered and swollen as to make breathing almost impossible. In this distressing condition the lion is unable to continue ordinary hunting of game, and when famished he prowls around villages. He invariably takes up his position near water, where he seizes the first person who comes along, kills him, and drags his prey to the nearest bush. Once he has discovered that it is an easy matter to kill human beings he is liable to become a confirmed man-eater.

One instance of a lion suffering extreme torture from quill-poisoning I encountered on the Zambesi. I had been out at night hunting hippo, about ten miles from my camp, and early the next morning some of my herd boys came to me and reported that the lions had stampeded all my cattle. They had followed them for five miles without reaching the marauders, so the boys urged me to hurry back and try to shoot the lions. I set out at daybreak with several natives to follow the trail. We had gone some distance when, just before reaching a native village, we found some of the cattle grazing. I told my boys to drive them between two thorn-trees so that I could count the beasts. The cattle passed one after the other, and, to my surprise, as the last ox came, a lion charged right from underneath the bush where I was standing. I grabbed my rifle, and the ox dashed away in terror. The lion swung round, charged me, and I shot him at four paces, blowing his head to pieces. This lion had suffered from extreme quill-poisoning; practically all his claws had gone, and the face and tongue were festering and rotting away.

The wounds and injuries inflicted by a man-eating lion are not necessarily great, but are generally fatal; indeed, I have seen no recovery, as virulent blood-poisoning sets in within twenty-four hours.

CHAPTER EIGHT

Tsetse Flies, Ants—and Elephants

THERE IS INTEREST, EXCITEMENT, and the zest of danger almost day by day in the wilds, and, of course, hundreds of episodes do not come into this spot-light I am throwing back into old Africa.

After the Zambesi the next arresting recollection is the time I spent with the Pygmies, who, to you probably, and certainly to me then, were almost legendary creatures, belonging to Grimm's tales or Gulliver rather than to actuality.

They are real enough — fascinating, primitive, naïve, brave, freakish. They live in a forest of bamboos on and around the active volcano of Sabinio, and of all the tribes I encountered in Africa their friendship was the hardest to win. But I managed to live with them for months.

Sabinio was a long way from Central Zambesia, and my wandering mood was all the time really leading my steps towards the Congo — that vast hidden land of shadows, so much of it untrodden, still secure to the wild things of the jungle, men and beasts. The trip brought me, among other sensations, my first sight of the sea. From Salisbury I went to Beira, where I purchased a ticket to Mombasa, for on my way I had made up my mind to see Kilimanjaro, the highest mountain in Africa. There I stayed a month marshalling my equipment, purchasing a large supply of provisions, tents, and calico for trading goods in the wilds; also a rifle and shot-gun. I then took train to Voi, a station on the recently completed Uganda Railway.

Tsetse Flies, Ants—and Elephants

I was advised that the best way to reach the mountain was to travel by donkey-wagon from Voi, and when I arrived at the foothills to continue with porters, I managed to secure two small wagons and donkey teams, and set off. Our adventures started the first day out. As darkness approached the donkeys refused to go any farther; they lay down in their harness and began rolling on the ground. We had entered a tsetse-fly belt.

It is incorrect to say that the tsetse does not bite at night; it does; and while during the day one can spot the tsetse, and so be prepared to protect oneself, at night the dread insect has its intended victim completely at its mercy. When natives are travelling they invariably walk in single file one behind the other, and in a fly belt each one is armed with a leafy branch, with which he hits any fly pitching on the back of the man in front. It is the unfriendly habit of the tsetse to secrete itself between the skin and the clothing, where it proceeds to suck the victim's blood into its body. The peculiar part is that the person bitten hardly, if ever, feels the injection of the probe and the consequent process of blood transfusion. I think that, as in the case of the vampire bat (found in the upper reaches of the Amazon river), the explanation is that the probe of the tsetse fly is coated with some chemical substance which has the effect of a local anæsthetic. As the fly sucks the blood, so its body gradually becomes distended until the stage is reached when it is gorged. It then commences to buzz, and finally emits a short "ping," rather like the safety valve blowing on a steam engine. That is the little siren that brings one to the alert, but in this case it is sounded after the danger, and not before. You will probably find and kill the fly, causing a stain of blood about the size of a shilling, but the damage has been done.

Hundreds of thousands of natives — perhaps millions — have been killed by the tsetse. I have often come to villages without a living soul in them; the inhabitants had died of sleeping sickness or had been driven out by the epidemic. On one occasion I stayed for more than a month on an island situated in Lake Nyanza, called Ukereve Island. When I revisited the island less than a year later there was not a single native left out of a population of some sixty thousand.

The natives amuse themselves by getting some one to take the fly off their bodies; then, holding the insect in their fingers, they tap it lightly on the head, which makes it draw in air. They continue this tapping until the fly is blown up like a balloon, and then let it go; they regard this as a form of punishment. Another method of native amusement is to decapitate the insect and then let it fly away headless. I once demonstrated these methods to General Smuts during the First World War, when I was acting as guide. We were travelling by motor car at the time, and entered a tsetse belt. The flies swarmed into the car, and we were constantly "shoo-ing" them away. My companions would not believe that the fly would flutter away headless. I caught one and removed its head, but unfortunately for me it did not fly away at all. The laugh was temporarily against me, until I suggested touching the fly — and away it went.

At first the symptoms of sleeping sickness are similar to those manifested in malaria; the victim suffers from severe headaches and fever, but later violent pains in the back of the neck are a sure symptom of sleeping sickness, and delirium sets in soon afterwards. During the primary stages of this terrible malady the sufferer develops a ravenous appetite, but as soon as he has satisfied his hunger he falls asleep, and perhaps for many hours remains in a state of coma, again craving food when he awakens.

We suffered no casualties on this occasion, and reached Kilimanjaro after eight days' travelling. Grand country, that held me for three months before I pushed on to Victoria

Nyanza. I arrived on the lake at an attractive spot called Port Florence. The first thing that impressed me there was that the natives, both men and women, went about absolutely naked, not even wearing loin-cloths as they did in the Zambesi valley. I asked some one why the aborigines were not made to wear loin-cloths, and was told that the Native Department had issued a lot of cloth free of charge for the purpose, but that the Kavirondo had appeared in the town shortly after with the material wound round their heads in turban style! The members of the Kavirondo tribe are very fit physically, and, in spite of, or more probably as a result of, being unclothed, they are most moral.

The difficulties of the trail before us were many. One night, when we were making for the south side of the lake, our camp was roused by the cry of "Ants." These cannibals of the insect world, advancing in billions in true military formation, had attacked us. They eat anything that comes in their path; indeed, so formidable are they that on one occasion a friend of mine had two goats completely devoured by them during the night; the next morning nothing but the polished bones remained. There is nothing to be done when red ants attack except to beat a hasty retreat; so we broke up camp and retired as fast as we could, while it rained continuously, and we were drenched to the skin. The red ant, however, is not without its uses, for it will destroy the white ant; I have seen them entering a nest of white ants, and emerging each with a white captive.

Part of our troubles was due to the fact that the rains that year were abnormal, and the whole country was just mud and water wherever we went. For days we struggled through a morass, until the porters with their heavy loads urged that we should cross a large inlet in dug-outs. This sheet of water was sixteen miles across and shallow, except in places where inland streams entered. It was quite possible to wade across most of the way. The surface was feathered by papyrus rushes, and we found that clusters of these were indicative of fairly deep water. As the porters could not walk through the papyrus with heavy loads, we constructed a raft by cutting down the papyrus. This clumsy structure was propelled by poling and towed by ropes. Ten days were occupied in crossing by such means, and we were wet through practically day and night during this time. Swarms of mosquitoes added to our discomfort, and so, at night, we pitched camp on termite ant-hills, which rose to enormous heights. We all contracted malaria very badly, but eventually reached dry land — beautiful tree country with granite kopjes dotted about, and everywhere thousands of cattle grazed. It was like coming out of Hades'into paradise.

The village we found here was called Mwanza, attractively situated on the shore; indeed, I liked the country so much that I purchased some land, secured Indian carpenters and native masons, and built a house. It was constructed of granite from the kopjes, and I obtained timber from the Ukereve Island, about thirty miles away, where there was some splendid African mahogany. Within four months the dwelling, consisting of five rooms, was completed. During this time I searched the district for a farm, and found an area which appealed to me. I purchased the property, which lay thirty-two miles out of "town" (white population one dozen!), and stocked it with four hundred head of cattle.

That didn't mean I had abandoned the Congo trip. Time counts for little in the sort of gipsy life I was leading — have always led. Nothing amazes me in busy towns so much as the hurry of countless people going somewhere — or nowhere — as if to waste a moment would be fatal. I was never a slave to the clock or calendar; only to the saucy hoyden Wanderlust. She always had me!

So while I lingered in Mwanza I was thinking of the next stage forward; gradually I prepared for the journey, and eventually left my new home and started off. For nearly three weeks we went north-west through wild country until we reached the Kagera. Since the opposite bank of this river was the Congo, the porters left us here and returned, though they first assisted in taking our goods across — a proceeding which occupied a full week. The river is deep and broad.

We had been unmolested, though doubtless watched — and as soon as we were established in this land of Ruanda I sent some of my personal boys with presents to the top of a near-by mountain, where, I learned, the local chief lived. These natives were said to be hostile, but my boys came back with the information that the chief had accepted my invitation to visit me. The next day he came, and when I saw his escort I wasn't so sure of his intentions. There is always the thrill of — anxiety, shall I call it? — in such moments. Six feet tall, with a magnificent silk shawl draped over one shoulder, this chief of the Watussi, with his armed guard, appeared formidable, for we were by now a small company. But his response to my greeting spoken in his own language was cordial, and all was well; when he heard that I had come to the Congo to hunt elephants he suggested that I should shoot them in his territory. I did not know there were elephants in that country, but the natives described a ravine where, they said, a herd of elephants had lived as long as it had been known. Former kings had hunted here occasionally with spears and poisoned arrows.

In due course we went to the place, and, almost at once, in a thicket I came on fresh spoor which led towards a mountain. Proceeding, I soon heard the familiar flapping of the ears, but the thicket was so dense that we could not see anything. I could, however, spot the whereabouts of the animals by the movement of the trees, and when I got on to the ground could see their legs; the rest of their bodies was invisible in the bush. At this moment the wind changed, the elephants got our scent, commenced trumpeting loudly, and charged off to another thicket three times as large as the first one we had entered; but by then it was too late in the day to pursue.

The next morning we went out again, taking one tent and the necessary provisions, and pitched camp on top of a hill overlooking the thicket. Again we picked up the spoor, and began following the beasts in a westerly direction along the ravine. It must have been about five o'clock when, once more, I decided to leave and carry on next day. I therefore handed my "500" express rifle to one of my boys and left the track. Suddenly, and quite unexpectedly, I was charged by an elephant bull that was already within a distance of twenty-five paces when I first saw him. I had only an 8-mm. rifle in my hand and was cornered. My boys had fled.

I fired four shots quickly at the elephant's head, but, as it was covered with bushes, my bullets had no effect. As I was ready to fire my fifth shot with the last cartridge in my magazine the elephant was almost on me, and I tried to dodge backward to reach the path. But I couldn't make it. His trunk reached out and I felt myself grabbed in the middle of the back — a most unpleasant sensation of sheer impotence, wriggling with one's arms and feet in the air. In that moment of crisis I was hardly aware that I still had my rifle — until, with a deafening roar, it went off. I had accidently pulled the trigger, and to that fortunate chance I probably owed my life. The elephant was about to toss me in the air, but the shot frightened him, and, instead of throwing me in front of him, as elephants usually do, he threw me backward. After all, that was pretty bad — for he tossed me about fifteen feet into the trees. The force with which I hit the branches stunned me for a while, and when I regained my senses I found I was covered with blood, and that my cheek had been torn open so widely that my teeth were exposed. The elephant had departed, and I was alone in the bush.

Although half blinded, I saw my rifle lying about two paces

away and tried to creep up to it, but just as I was on the point of reaching the weapon an elephant cow came right on top of me. I lay quite still, and she passed without noticing me. Immediately after this another cow appeared, and it was only when she had also passed that I was able to secure my rifle, slip in a cartridge, and follow. I came up with the beast and placed a shot in the spine. The first elephant must have heard this, and came blundering back, trumpeting and ready to charge again. I was now in the path which we had previously cut, and endeavored to get out of the way. When the elephant approached me he first charged, then commenced tearing up trees, trampling the ground, and finally, after trumpeting loudly, followed the others.

I was bleeding profusely from a cut above the eye; had it been slightly lower I might have lost my eye altogether. I therefore thought I would return in a different direction and reach camp as soon as I could. Walking through the thicket was a terrible ordeal, for soon it was as black as pitch, and my only guide was my bushman's sense of direction. I struggled along until about eleven o'clock, when I saw the camp-fires. The natives were all sitting round the burning logs, and were thunderstruck at seeing me as they thought I had been killed.

Ruanda was ruled by a king named Msinga, and one of his relatives was Chief Semahari, whom I met. It was amusing to see these native lords. They never walked; wherever they went they were carried in chairs rather resembling a child's perambulator. These vehicles were made entirely of grass, with long wooden poles projecting on each side as grips for the carriers. The Watussi are a very arrogant race possessing enormous herds of cattle, in which they take great pride. They will not permit any person outside their tribe even to herd their cattle with their own beasts, or to take part in their feasts, or join the retinue of the chiefs.

Semahari and I got on well, and he accompanied me some

distance on my journey. I found him a most admirable guide and philosopher. Sometimes he came to my tent and sat for hours, while all his followers squatted round listening to our conversation. He told me many interesting tales concerning his people. None of their kings, he declared, ever died a natural death; it was expected of them that, when it was considered that they had reigned sufficiently long, they should take poison in order to make way for a successor.

He told me how the tribe had migrated from the north, and eventually had conquered the Bahutu race of the country, and had settled here. They regarded conquered races as slaves who had no right to own cattle, but were entitled, as a privilege, to possess goats and sheep. The Watussi did no hoeing or harvesting; cultivation was left to the Bahutu, who had to do as they were told, otherwise their lives were forfeit.

Both the men and women were good-looking, with skins of extremely fine texture, good features, and straight noses. The women had beautiful hands with tapering fingers, whose only function in life was to attend to the cooking. Their diet consisted of mealie meal, kaffir corn, manna beans of several types, and, of course, bananas, which grew wild and in profusion all over the country. The Watussi women did not gather them; even that labor had to be performed by the Bahutu.

Each man could have as many wives as he could afford, bought in exchange for cattle, and when a marriage ceremony was celebrated every one was invited. The Watussi did not employ drums except when mustering the men for war. Their music was produced by flutes and stringed instruments. The sound of the flutes would carry for long distances, and when they had their dances the melody was enchanting. Semahari travelled with me for a month, and during all that time he never ate nor drank from any utensil but his own, and would not eat the food prepared by my own men. They were splendid athletes, swift runners and marvellous jumpers, who could easily clear six feet six inches. Leaping is, in fact, a national pastime of, these aristocratic savages. Some of their picked athletes will clear a jump of over seven feet, which easily eclipses all white men's records.

When I was staying at Semahari's village the natives told me that a lion had caught a wild pig in their gardens, which were about one hundred yards away from the village and were situated on the edge of a swamp of high grass and reeds. With two boys and my shot-gun I proceeded to the spot, and found that the lion had dragged its prey into the reeds. Presently we could distinctly hear the animal eating, and I stole towards the spot expecting that the animal would charge, but instead of that he decamped into some other reeds. Some of the Watussi crossed the swamp, and stood in a long row with their bows-and-arrows and assegais. I ventured into the reeds and flushed the lion. The beast roared and cleared off through the swamp towards the Watussi, but when he came to within forty yards of them, instead of charging, he swerved, and made an effort to regain the reeds. I saw one of the men release his bow, and then the lion jumped into the air, and, after tottering for a few paces, stood with an arrow projecting from one shoulder. He took the point of the arrow between his teeth, extricated it, and then jumped back into the swamp. I pursued him with my shot-gun, but before I reached him he fell dead. The arrow, poisoned of course, had gone right through the soft part of the shoulder without striking any bones, and had emerged on the other side. I have often wondered what poison the Watussi steeped their arrows in; whatever it was, it was extremely effective.

I was sorry when we parted company, he to return, I to push on to Sabinio, that impressive volcano which lies beside the placid waters of Kivu, highest, healthiest, and most beautiful of all the Central African lakes. The height of the crater is thirteen thousand feet; it is a tremendous climb, for there are few rocks. The red volcanic mud gives it its name Sabinio, or Soapy, yet we found nimble-footed elephants almost on top. Here, too, is the habitat of the gorilla.

In my ascent of Sabinio I did not enter the bush at once, for I was told by the natives in the surrounding district that Pygmies lived inside the bamboos, and that these little people were intensely hostile. I pitched my camp at the edge of the bamboo, hard by a little pool where the elephants came frequently to drink. But my objective at this time was not so much hunting as to induce the Pygmies to make friends with me; I was desperately keen to see how these tiny people lived. For a month I sent messengers from the neighboring villages — natives who had got to know the little folk, traded with them, and knew their language — but my efforts to establish contacts were without success. The messengers took presents of goats and sheep, and they also took some risks, for the Pygmies were far from friendly. Eventually the Pygmies would come to within fifty yards of my camp, and we exchanged messages. Then one day they sent word to the effect that the following day a number of their men, women, and children would stand at a distance so that I might see them.

About fifty yards from my tent was a little mound of lava, and here it was that they arranged to congregate. I swore that I would not attack or try to capture them. The next morning twenty or more men, women, and children came out of the bamboos and climbed on to the little mound, while I sat in a deck-chair in front of my tent with an interpreter standing next to me. I asked the little people to come to my tent and have a meal, and pointed out to them sheep and goats which were grazing around the camp, but they laughed and said that, obviously, I wanted to catch them. All the time the men were standing with their bows ready to shoot, and when I showed them that my hands were empty and I was quite unarmed, two men came to the camp, and the sheep were brought. I said that unless they had a meal with me they could not take anything back to the others. Among the sheep two small goats were caught, and we handed one of these to the little men. The Pygmies still had their bows-and-arrows and spears ready, but when they were handed the goat one of them seized it in both hands and held it down by the forelegs, while the other plunged his assegai into the animal's throat, and, while it was still kicking, a Pygmy cut off a piece with his assegai and ate it, then sliced off a piece for his friend; and they proceeded with their feast, eating the entire carcase, hair and all.

The Pygmies are about four feet high, well built and sturdy, with strong arms and chests, and their faces are broad with huge noses. They do not wear clothing of any description, and never cook their food. The contact created by means of the goat made intercourse easier, and soon they permitted me into the bamboos and showed me their habitations. Within a week most of them were following me everywhere, like pets, and protested that when I left they were coming too. As a matter of fact, quite a company of them did.

CHAPTER NINE

Among the Pygmies: A Fight in the Bush

FOR KILLING THE ELEPHANT these little people have special sharp spears which are made by neighboring tribes, and are obtained by the bartering of ivory. The blade is twenty inches long and nearly three inches wide, and the top end of the handle is weighted with iron, ending in a sharp point.

I had the experience of seeing hunts in Pygmy-land on several occasions, and this is what took place. A large number of the little folk crept up to the elephant in the middle of the day, while the beast was asleep, and, within ten yards of it, noiselessly dug their spears into the ground by the sharp, weighted end, with the blades all pointing at an angle in the direction of the sleeping elephant. When the weapons were in a row the party divided into two lines, one half standing on each side with their assegais ready. The elephant, still unaware of danger, continued to slumber, and then one man was sent through the row of spears planted in the ground. He crept along to the sleeping beast, clapped his hands, and shouted, disturbing the elephant, which, alarmed, immediately charged the man as he ran back between the spears. The two parties from the right and left then jumped in and stabbed the animal. Rarely did an elephant escape; the spears planted in the ground do not do much damage, but the animal is hampered by them, and the moment the Pygmies see this they charge from all sides.

When the elephant is dead the whole tribe dance round the carcase, and it is a really revolting sight to witness the feast. I describe it briefly because, after all, it is a sidelight on what curious things happen in that world of half-light where savages still dwell. Entire families arrive, make shelters from the bamboos, and stay until the gorging is over. Each gourmand helps himself, cutting off pieces and devouring them at once. The Pygmies enter right inside the stomach and sit there, guzzling the entrails, which are the favorite tit-bits.

Pygmies are cunning, and know the value of ivory — they had seen Arab traders buying tusks from the adjoining tribes. One day a deputation from them informed me that they had a big pair of tusks which they wanted to sell, so I told them to bring the ivory to my camp. They replied they could not do this, since their trading custom was that one or two envoys of the purchaser should go with them to inspect the ivory. They then announced that before the two boys could inspect I must give them calico, and they indicated by means of sticks laid end to end the number of yards they wanted. They also asked for blankets and beads. When the articles of barter were produced the Pygmies laid them on the ground and said that for a blanket you get a goat, and then converted their bargaining into goats. After all this palaver it was estimated that fifty goats would be the inspection fee.

My men went with the Pygmies, and came back saying that they had seen the tusks, but had not been allowed to touch them. Naturally I wanted to know the weight, and the Pygmies, well aware of this, made it the occasion for more bartering with blankets, beads, and calico — reconverting the goods into goats, and arranging that my men could take the measurements, so that I could guess fairly well at the weight and estimate the value. Eventually, when I obtained the tusks, I had paid almost as much as the price at the coast! That was the last of my ivory trading with the Pygmies — they drove too hard a bargain!

In this country I did some elephant-hunting, and found the Pygmies splendid trackers and absolutely fearless. The elephants in Sabinio lived on the bamboo, breaking down the young shoots, which are sweet and soft. The gorilla, who also dwells in those parts, persistently follows in the wake of the elephants and feeds on his leavings.

Once the Pygmies were on the spoor they kept close on the heels of the animal they were tracking, and confusion often arose from the fact that it was almost impossible to tell the difference between the footmark of a gorilla and that of a Pygmy; indeed, the little folk themselves often could not tell until they came to wet ground. When approaching an elephant the Pygmies would not allow me to fire until the gorillas were out of the way; they were very superstitious on this point. The great apes make a chuckling noise as they move along, and the Pygmies would whistle when approaching them. The moment the whistling commenced the gorillas would decamp.

I have a vivid memory of my first encounter with a gorilla. One morning my bearer roused me with the information that there was fresh spoor of a herd of elephants which had passed near the camp at an early hour. I hastily donned my clothes, reached for rifle and ammunition, and summoned two of the best Pygmy trackers. We had not proceeded very far on the track of the herd before it was apparent that a huge gorilla had also taken up the trail. At the time a dense mist enveloped most of the bush, and the knowledge that the huge ape was between us and our quarry slowed up our progress considerably, as we had no desire to be taken unawares by this powerful beast. The Pygmies again and again whistled and trilled, in an attempt to scare the gorilla off, but with no effect. They actually created so much din that I feared that the herd we were tracking would decamp.

As we had already had a long and arduous chase, my patience became exhausted, and I told the Pygmies to lead me towards the gorilla, as I intended to shoot it. They were terrified. If I shot the gorilla, they chattered, our lives would be endangered, for its mates would emerge from the surrounding bush and tear us to shreds. This warning was accompanied by a most vivid description in pantomime of what would happen when the gorillas arrived. The only effect of all this was to arouse my hunter's curiosity to fever heat, and I determined, if possible, to have a closer view of one of these giant apes. We quickened our pace, and, after about half an hour, it was apparent from the feel of some freshly chewed bamboo shoots that we were in close proximity to the man-ape.

My guides now proceeded with the greatest caution, and, watching them, I realized what wonderful bushmen they really were. They each moved through the bush as silently and stealthily as a leopard. Suddenly they halted and became rigid, and I crept to them as quietly as I could. They had worked right round the gorilla. We were standing in a clump of bamboos, and the first thing I noticed was that the air was tainted with an acrid, animal smell. One Pygmy gently parted the bamboos, and, to this day, there is indelibly etched on my brain a picture which, I am sure, would cause many a child to have nightmares for the rest of its life. I looked out on a clearing in the bush, roughly about fifty yards in diameter, where the bamboos had been trampled flat by the herd of elephants. In the centre of the clearing sat a huge hairy object lighted up fitfully by the sun, which was now beginning to penetrate the mists. A huge head turned towards our direction, and one of the most diabolical faces I have ever seen held me spellbound; a face with no forehead, huge, overhanging eyebrows, two small, close-set eyes, glinting redly, a flattened nose with large nostrils, and, finally, a huge slit of a mouth, bulging with teeth. The unprepossessing beast was chewing the young shoots from the bamboos torn down by the elephants. I was absolutely fascinated by the ogre, and was only brought back to reality when the wind wafted to my senses a most pungent animal smell which caused both my nostrils and my throat to smart. Slowly I raised my rifle, aiming at the base of the skull, and as I pressed the trigger the beast collapsed without a murmur.

My guides stood stock-still, and the expression on their faces was something to remember — a mixture of terror, awe, and exultation. I suddenly realized that I was feeling extremely uncomfortable, and that my clothes were sodden with perspiration. We stepped out of the clearing, and at close quarters the odor from the great beast was almost overpowering. The shot had thrown the gorilla on to its belly, and it took the united efforts of the two Pygmies, my bearer, and myself to turn the body on its back.

I made an examination of it. From the top of its head to the soles of its feet it measured an inch or two over six feet. Its arms were extremely long, powerful, and thick, and I noticed that there was hardly any taper from the shoulders to the wrists. The head was enormous, and seemed to fit right into a socket between the shoulders, with little or no neck. The chest was like a barrel, and the belly was monstrous — distending the skin and, to a large extent, obscuring the powerful but short legs. The whole body, except the chest, was enveloped in thick, matted dark-brown hair of a very coarse texture. The hands, I noted, were remarkably like my own. The lower lip sagged and exposed a formidable array of teeth, while the jaw itself protruded. The general effect of the head was a continual backward slope from the jaw to the eyebrow, then a flattening out, and a final rounding of the skull.

I had spent a long time examining the gorilla, and, abandoning the elephants, we returned to camp. In a very short time the jabbering among the Pygmies indicated that the two trackers were telling the story of the kill. My bearer told me that the Pygmies were definite that, had the shot not killed the gorilla outright, the consequent howling and beating on the chest of the wounded beast would have caused several others to appear on the scene with bad results to ourselves. Many a time during the day, when I was at camp, I heard noises similar to those made by the natives' war-drums, which were taken up and repeated in various other parts of the forest. They were caused by gorillas beating their chests, and I came to the conclusion that, like war-drums, these were means of communication or warning.

At the time of which I write both Europeans and natives regarded the gorilla as a most ferocious and dangerous animal, liable to attack any hunter on sight.

After remaining with the Pygmies for three months I departed from this amazingly interesting country (in which I shot six elephants and one gorilla), for my mode of life was becoming precarious. The Belgian Government was virtually at war with cannibal tribes which began to invade the country adjoining that of the Pygmies and German East Africa.

I intended to travel to Ruwenzori, the shy and most elusive mountain range in Eastern Africa. When I was ready to start nearly a hundred of the Pygmies, men, women, and children, persisted in accompanying me and my goats and cattle. Proceeding northward, I once again pitched camp on the Kagera. This river, by the way, supplies the greatest source of water to the Victoria Nyanza.[1] The natives told me that the water in the river was always bubbling up, but it was cool and pleasant to drink. The source of the Nile was said to be here, so I made up my mind to go all along the Ruanga and see for myself. On reaching the source I found it was actually a mineral spring, and not far from this spot I noticed a very large native village. Here, I thought, would be excellent opportunities for

[1] The Kagera river is in reality the most remote headstream of the Nile. The sources of its principal upper branch, the Nyavarongo stream, rise in the hills immediately to the east of Lake Kivu. After meandering for more than four hundred miles the Kagera enters the Victoria Nyanza just south of the equator. The river was first heard of by Speke, who, with Grant, discovered the Victoria Nyanza, and was reached by him in January, 1862, in his effort to discover the Nile source.

trading, and I decided to make my camp. I sent the usual presents to the chief, but, after waiting for more than an hour, my men returned with my gifts, stating that the chief did not want to accept anything, nor did he desire us to be near his village. Indeed, he threatened war unless we departed.

It was a large location, and, deeming discretion to be the better part of valor, we departed in a north-westerly direction, passing behind the village; at the head of a small lake, which we reached at sunset, I selected a spot for the camp. My cook and some of the boys went to fetch water, and came back with the information that there were many dead and mutilated people lying near the water, and that there was no live person to be seen. Darkness was coming on, and despite the ominous surroundings I fell asleep. The next morning before leaving I went to the water to investigate, and saw the heads and multilated bodies of sixteen natives; plainly, this was the work of the cannibals.

We had hardly started on our trek that day before my porters informed me that the chief who had refused my presents was following us with hundreds of men. I sent word to him advising him to retire, but he continued his pursuit. At that time we were climbing mountains — which the natives scaled with the aid of pointed sticks, for the footpaths were extremely slippery — and some of the boys made footholds by wriggling their big toes into the ground. After many hours of ascent we reached a plateau, where the country was open, treeless, and covered with short grass, and here we halted. On our left, a couple of miles away, was a bamboo forest, while ahead of us was a big kloof. We saw hundreds of natives taking up their positions on the far side of this kloof; they were the people who had followed us, and they settled down within a quarter of a mile of the camp. Their leader shouted and warned us to turn back. I shouted back defiantly, and they charged in the direction of the camp.

Among the Pygmies: A Fight in the Brush

They were led by a witch-doctor, rigged out in his war-dress, covered from head to foot with skins and feathers, who came careering down the mountain, and, although I warned him that if he did not stop I would shoot, he dashed forward, followed by many others. The situation was desperate, so I fired. The witch-doctor dropped instantly. This had a deterrent effect upon the others; immediately they saw their medicine man was killed they stopped. I threatened to shoot again unless they departed. They went away, and we continued along the top of the kloof, where I found three more bodies carved up in the manner of the mutilations I had observed at the edge of the water in the morning.

In the afternoon we came to a large native village, where banana groves and gardens were to be seen on the slopes of the hills. I sent for the chief as soon as I entered the village, and he came forward in a friendly manner. I asked him to sell me two oxen in exchange for calico, and within a few minutes the oxen arrived. Meanwhile my camp had been pitched for the night, and, as I was tired, I lay down, after instructing my head-man to give one of the oxen to the Pygmies and to kill the remaining animals for the other natives.

Soon a great noise of laughter arose. I got up, and from the entrance of my hut called to my head-man to ascertain the cause. He replied that the people were laughing at the Pygmies. I looked out on a revolting sight. I saw the Pygmies congregated round the ox — which had only been stunned — and they were cutting off chunks of meat from the live animal, which was on its back struggling and kicking. I felt inclined to thrash the lot of them, and accordingly shouted that if this kind of barbarism occurred again they would have to return. I promptly ordered one of my boys to kill the beast, and returned to my tent; but within half an hour I heard more laughter, followed by a tremendous outburst of shouting and war-cries from the villagers. Naturally I felt somewhat alarmed, and, taking my revolver, went to investigate. The Pygmies had gone into the native gardens and had helped themselves to green peas, pulling out the plants, roots and all, while the natives of the village were fighting them with bows-and-arrows.

Pandemonium reigned, and if I had left the Pygmies alone they would, I am sure, have won. It was a grotesque sight to see them covered from head to foot with green-pea plants which they were carrying from the gardens they had raided. I stopped the fight and managed to make peace with the chief, who agreed to accept payment in calico for the damage done. I was furious with the Pygmies, and told them so; their reply was that they were hungry, and the peas were good food — a very simple but dangerous philosophy! I again returned to bed in comparative peace, but shortly before midnight I was disturbed by moans and groans of agony from the Pygmies. All night long this continued, and in the morning five of my small but pugnacious friends were dead. They had gorged themselves with peas, which later had become distended in their stomachs, and had caused intense pain. I told them it was impossible to continue any farther with me, and that they must return to the bamboos. They agreed, on the condition that I sent an armed escort with them. There was some justification in their attitude, so I sent some of my boys with them, and waited in camp. I also presented the Pygmies with goats for food, to take them as far as the bamboo forest, and I gave three of the boys rifles. On the evening of the second day my boys returned and declared that, as soon as they reached the bamboo forest, the Pygmies told them they could go back, as they would be safe.

I now changed my direction to the north-west and struggled through more bamboo forest, after a while emerging in open country. In three hours we came to a big swamp with bamboo forests on either side. The morass was so deep and treacherous that in places we sank in mud nearly up to our thighs. We eventually crossed this bad patch, reached the bamboos, and followed a native path for a mile into open country, where we found a small lake and a deserted village. While camp was being pitched some of my boys who had been sent to fetch water dashed back, saying that they had been attacked and that my cook and four boys had been killed at the water. I sent my head-boy to investigate, but I never saw him again, for almost as soon as he had gone hundreds of natives charged down on the camp from all directions. My boys stampeded, and several of them were killed. The warriors came into my camp, tore my tent to pieces, took all my kit, and began dividing it. I retreated with the survivors of my safari in the direction from which we had come. I had been robbed of everything, and noticed that the natives had yards and yards of calico wrapped round their heads. They tried to surround us, and my plight was terrible, for I had very little ammunition. I defended myself with a shot-gun, firing at the leaders. I was then to realize that I had put my trust in a cheap and useless weapon. Cornered, I fired several shots in quick succession, when suddenly the seam between the barrels melted and the barrels separated.

That left only one course open, flight — an ignominious situation where natives are the enemy. I and five remaining boys got into the bamboos, running as hard as we could, with hundreds of savages in pursuit. We stumbled into an elephant track which crossed our way and darted along this, having the intense satisfaction of hearing our pursuers pass us by, maintaining the original course. We were saved temporarily, but still defenseless, except for a Mauser pistol with seven rounds of ammunition. When darkness fell we descended the mountain, crossed the morass, and slept. Continuing our flight, we again reached the bamboos while it was still dark, and we could hear elephants breaking down the reeds. At daybreak

I looked down upon the valley of savagery where I had seen
the sixteen heads. I saw that it was thickly populated, and as
the inhabitants were enemies we kept in hiding.

Then came an episode poignantly tragic. At noon we
observed a score of my porters coming along the old road.
They were easily distinguishable, for they were clad in calico,
whereas the local natives wore kilts made from very pliable
grass which grew profusely in this region. As soon as I spotted
my boys I feared that they would be killed. They entered the
village, and it seemed at first as if they met with an amicable
reception, for they sat down and had a palaver inside a stockade. Presently more natives began to gather round them, and
quite suddenly we saw the flashing of spears and heard
screams. They were all brutally murdered before my eyes,
and I was powerless to help. It was one of the most distressing
moments of my life.

When darkness fell we retraced our steps and began to
make back in the direction of the Victoria Nyanza, which was
at least four hundred miles distant. We decided to keep in
hiding during the day, and travel at night, when we could help
ourselves to anything edible in the gardens. For eight days and
nights we rationed ourselves in this manner. It was winter and
the nights were cold — indeed a nightmare trek. At last we
again reached the Watussi country and food in plenty.

In the first village I entered I was informed that a German
officer was at the capital of King Msinga with many askaris,
and that they were looking for me.

CHAPTER TEN

The Prussian Heel

IT TOOK me eight days to make Msinga's village, and here I found the officer, Vryherr Oberleutnant von Nordryk. Having given an account of my luckless safari, I asked his help to recover my equipment and cattle from the natives. Not only did he refuse assistance; he dictatorially announced that I could lay no claim to them.

"I hold German licenses to enter the country to shoot and trade," I answered him, " and I shall report the whole matter to the British Government."

"Do as you like," he laughed contemptuously.

It was only later on that I learned this Oberleutnant had received information that I had killed a number of natives, and he had sent a runner to obtain a warrant for my arrest.

In just over a week I reached Bukoba, a German town on the west shores of Victoria Nyanza, but I was so ill with malaria that I could proceed no farther by land. Procuring two large dug-outs from Paramount Chief Gahiki, who lived just outside the town, we therefore continued by water. For three days we paddled on, but by then I was prostrate with fever and saw no alternative but to send a message to the German authorities at Mwanza (on the shores of the lake, not far away), asking for a Government boat to fetch me from the island where we had pitched camp. Shortly after sunrise the next morning the German steamer approached the island. Aboard the vessel, as it drew near, I recognized three officials I had met before, Captain Hoffman-Siegfreit — in full uniform — Dr. Albori, and Sergeant Schubert. They landed and came straight up to my tent, where I was lying down. Hoffman-Siegfreit shook hands with me and then broke the news in faltering English: "My friend, I am very sorry, but it is my duty to arrest you for shooting forty-seven natives." He told me also that my property had been confiscated by the Government pending the hearing of the case. I assured him my acts had been in self-defense and that I was ready to face any trial. I wonder whether my words would have come so readily had I known the long-drawn-out affair that awaited. They took me to hospital, and I was there for almost a month while Dr. Albori attended me. One morning, while I was in hospital, a German judge, who introduced himself as Dr. Neumann, arrived, and after telling me not to sit up asked me to relate what had happened. He spoke good English, and I told him my whole story in detail — a labor which occupied two days, for I was still very weak and had to rest every now and then

What a wearying business that trial was ! I was taken down to Dar-es-Salaam and jailed. The bitterness of those months — the sheer unfairness of it all — still makes me hot, but all that need be said here is that for nearly a year I was kept in prison while inquiries were being made way back in the jungle, and then, when I was released on bail, the case hung on more months, until I had been held up for two whole years while lawyers and Governments argued. In the end they gave me a sentence of twelve months, I suppose to save "face" — for they admitted what I had done had been in self-defense; and as I had been so long under detention I walked out of court a free man. The one benefit I reaped through it all was that I learned to speak German.

At once I made inquiries concerning my property, and received a severe blow when I was told that my cattle — 774 head altogether — had been taken away by the German Government, and sold for a hundred and fifty pounds ! Their paltry excuse was that rinderpest had broken out, and when my cattle began to die the Government thought it better to

"Unexpectedly I was charged by an elephant bull" (see p. 110)

Photo South African Railways and Harbours

"The leopard . . . . selects a well above eyelevel", p. 142

sell the beasts quickly and retrieve something. I had to take
what was given to me, and when my hotel and legal expenses
were paid I was nearly penniless. There was just enough cash
to buy an ordinary 8-mm. Mauser rifle, but there was no
money for equipment and a supply of provisions.

I had to start life all over again.

It was then I went to the Rufiji, scene of many adventures in
later years, one of which — the ending of the *Königsberg* — I
have already recounted. So meagrely equipped was I that I
felt ashamed to say I was going to hunt elephants. I had no
tent and hardly any provisions — just a few blankets and a
rifle. I told my friends that I was wandering off for the week-
end in quest of hippo.

With five natives I left Dar-es-Salaam on October 27, 1906,
and after travelling through very hilly country and dense
scrubby bush, thickly populated by natives, we reached the
Rufiji. The tribes living in the mountainous country were
known as the Bassazuru, and were great cultivators, growing
principally the "mohoko," which has a root rather like a sweet-
potato. The plant itself is sometimes as much as seven feet
high, and its enormous roots can be used in a variety of ways,
chiefly for making arrowroot.

We found the natives on the Rufiji in extreme terror on
account of man-eating lions. They would not dare to leave
their huts after four o'clock, and were even afraid to go into
their gardens, for if the lions had not invaded the huts during
the night they would lie in wait in the mealie fields. It was the
native rebellion of 1904, already referred to, that had set up
these conditions; I don't suppose anywhere in Africa was a
district so full of man-eating lions. They had, so to speak, been
reared to the taste of human flesh, and hunted little else.

The natives begged me to save them from the reign of terror
under which they shuddered. Their huts were well built, with
mud walls, but they had become so devastated by fear that

numbers went into one abode at night, and barricaded themselves in to prevent the door from being burst open. I told them to report to me each morning if anyone had been killed, and promised that we would make a drive. I advised them not to barricade themselves in the huts, but to make fires in the doorways, take it in turn to keep guard, and as soon as a lion was seen by the light of the fire to throw pieces of burning wood at the beast, which would frighten him away.

The natives persisted, however, in barricading themselves in, and one morning a frightened deputation reported to me that seventeen people had been killed in one hut during the night.

On investigation I heard a story of stark terror from one of the survivors. The previous evening, as usual, the natives barred themselves in, and during the night a lion made several attempts to break down the door, eventually jumping to the fragile roof, which collapsed under its weight. The inmates all started screaming and crashing themselves against the walls in a maddened effort to escape, but there was no exit except through the barricaded doorway. In their terror they were unable to burst through this quickly enough. You can imagine the nightmare scene — those cowering, dodging savages with a mad lion amok among them rushing from one end of the scrummaging group to the other, killing indiscriminately until eventually one man managed to remove enough of the barricade to get at the door. The first out was the lion! Not one of the bodies had been taken away or eaten, which proved that the lion had been so maddened with fear that he had forgotten his hunger.

We made one or two drives, and we killed several of tne man-eaters; then I had to move on, for I was anxious to obtain ivory, because money was an absolute necessity to me then. It was the finest elephant-hunting ground I have ever encountered in Africa, since the herds were running separately, the bulls being concentrated together away from the cows. These bulls were in bodies of ten or twelve, and of all ages. I estimate the age of the elephant, by the way, from observations I had made; for I tamed seven which I had caught in different districts. On the average their ivory grew at the maximum rate of three-quarters of a pound to a pound in each tusk in a year. Taking that as an estimate, the age of an elephant with tusks weighing two hundred and fifty pounds each must be very great. My longest tusks were nine feet three inches, each weighing a hundred and twenty pounds. A long one never weighs as much as a short, thick tusk. Of the latter I have obtained specimens a hundred and sixty pounds in weight, with a length of only eight feet.

In a few months, poorly equipped as I was, I shot my way back to a more or less established position. I had collected sufficient ivory to send a runner to Dar-es-Salaam and bring me back all the provisions I wanted, together with a decent tent, and more important, a new rifle. Of the many kills I made during that time there were one or two episodes outside the hunter's routine. Here, first, is the story of one old tusker whose end remains rather vividly in my memory.

I had been out, and on returning picked up his spoor — noticing that the line of his tracks was in the direction of camp. We reached dense bamboos, where it was difficult to see more than five paces ahead, and had it not been for elephant tracks we should have been compelled to cut our way through. After we had gone another three miles we heard a noise like the buzzing of thousands of bees, and for a while dispersed in different directions in quest of honey. I proceeded to the spot from which the greatest noise emanated. It was in a clearing of bamboos, and there I found thousands of blue-bottle flies swarming on an elephant's head. The animal got our wind and charged, and I ran for my life, for I had no rifle. My boy rushed after me and quickly handed me the Mauser.

Jungle Man

The elephant stood, and I cautiously approached and tried to put in a vital shot, but each time he detected my movements, and with his extraordinarily acute hearing, he came towards me. Finally he charged again, and I maneuvered him into an open spot where there was a rain-pool. He stood at the edge of the bamboos, and I whispered to one of my boys that he must entice the elephant to charge again by running past me into the open, so that I could get in a telling shot. These tactics succeeded, and I placed a bullet through the ear, which dropped him dead immediately.

That poor beast, I found, had been shot before — by native hunters — and an iron slug had penetrated close to the eye, just where the tusks commence to grow. Here was an immense festering sore, and it was this that had attracted the filthy flies. When we extracted the tusks we found a piece of iron more than an inch long. On one side there were actually seven splintered tusks, each with a separate nerve, all growing towards one another in the form of a cluster. When the skull was opened it was disclosed that the iron had penetrated the tusk splitting it into these seven pieces, and each piece grew separately with individual nerves. The unfortunate beast had probably suffered this injury five or six years previously, and since then must have been in constant agony.

Then there was the day I cracked with a damaged ankle and one of my favorite boys was killed. Six boys and I, with provisions for the day and with well-filled water-bottles, set off cutting in for spoor, when we reached the tracks of two large bulls. As this part of the country was under the banks of an old course of the Rufiji river the elephant grass was high and thick, and in a wet season, especially after rain, was so wet that a safari, however short, meant being drenched to the skin. Even the dew remains for hours on this grass, and in such country elephant-tracking is not difficult to an experienced hunter, who can tell from the signposts of the bush how close the animals are. If the grass is still wet then you know the beasts have passed hours previously; and if there is no dew it is an indication that they are near. In this case the elephants had passed during the earlier portion of the night, and the grass was wet. After we had proceeded a mile the native in advance was stopped in his path by a big snake, which he immediately dispatched. Natives are extremely superstitious with regard to serpents, and the rest of the boys severely reprimanded the man for killing a snake.

"Don't you know that one of us will be killed?" they chorused in dismay.

Another quaint superstition in connection with elephant-hunting is that if a man is charged by a beast it is a sure sign that his wife is committing adultery, and no matter how many miles he may be from his home he will return to his hut and severely beat the unfaithful spouse.

Two miles farther on we entered a dry river-bed covered with dense thorn-bush known in South Africa as the haak-stick. On the north bank there were old native gardens, throughout which were scattered large marula-trees, which provide a favorite fruit of the elephant. Presently we spotted two elephants about a hundred yards from the bank, and we cautiously picked our way between them and the bush. When we were within fifty yards they got our wind, and I fired. The shot entered the head of one, who, although he dropped immediately on his knees, nevertheless rose again and charged.

The frontal shot is usually ineffectual, as, on account of the thickness of the skull, it is a matter of pure luck if the quarry is dropped. From the base of the trunk to the brain is nearly three feet, and the brain is comparatively small and situated at the back of the head, encased in the thinnest part of the skull.

When this particular bull, screaming with rage and pain,

was within five paces I had to race for safety as my shots had
failed to stop him. There was a big tree on an ant-hill round
which I ran, and the elephant, waving his trunk, tried to get
my scent. I reloaded and cautiously emerged from cover, but
the beast heard me and charged again, and this time I once
more hit him in the forehead. Still he came on, screaming and
waving his trunk with rage. It is a terrifying sensation when an
elephant is on your heels, for you imagine that at any moment
he is going to reach out with his trunk and throw you in the
air. One boy dashed in front of me, and the next thing I knew
was that I was knocked down, while the elephant had passed
over me and was still chasing the native. When I tried to get
to my feet there was nasty pain in my right ankle, which I
thought was broken; it was, however, only dislocated. The
screaming continued, and I realized that the boy was still
being pursued, but presently the native entered the scattered
trees, and the elephant passed him by.

In such circumstances it is unwise to whistle, for the
elephant is extremely sagacious and, no matter what bird-
noise is imitated, it seems to be able to distinguish the human
note, and will return to the charge. When I thought the
elephant had departed I whistled quietly, and one boy, named
Juma, reached my side; he said that if it had not been for
reaching the bush he would have been killed.

I remained at this spot for the rest of the day, waiting for
the remainder of the natives, but they did not return, and in
the meantime I made a crude splint for my dislocated ankle.
I took two pieces of bark cut from a tree, and tied them very
tightly around the damaged ankle. I had often seen the natives
do this, for the African aborigines are adepts at making splints.
On one occasion which I recall a woman broke her leg when
a falling tree struck her. I suggested she should be taken to the
nearest hospital, but the natives assured me that their own
medicine man would fix the broken limb. Presently the mouti

(medicine) man arrived with a knife and an axe. He cut two large pieces of bark and some fine strips of the same material, and, using the slats for bandages, spliced the woman's leg. This done, he asked me to provide a big rooster, and said that to get the woman healed he must also break the rooster's leg. I gave him an old cockerel, and the medicine man then broke the bird's leg in two, immediately splicing it in the same manner as the woman's leg. It was so well done that the bird tripped off at once, limping but otherwise unperturbed. The woman was then sent away to another district.

"Watch the rooster," said the doctor. "As soon as its leg is healed the woman will be cured."

When the fowl was able to get about without limping the splints were removed. "Now I go to get wife," announced the boy with perfect confidence. Sure enough, she was quite recovered. Most African natives are wonderful at bone-setting, and the whole operation is done without the aid of any opiate.

My ankle pained me, so that I stayed, hoping for the boys to return and make a hammock; but they did not, and we made preparations for the night. Juma disappeared into the bush to fetch water, and suddenly I heard the screaming of an elephant and at once guessed that it was the wounded beast which had chased us in the morning. From the noise of the crashing bush, the trumpeting of the elephant, and the shouts of the native I could tell that the elephant was pursuing the boy, and that he was fleeing towards me. And there was I, unarmed, with a badly dislocated ankle. When they emerged from the bush I noticed that the elephant's trunk was stretched out and was almost touching the boy's head. Juma saw me, realized he was bringing the elephant on to me, and swerved, dropping the water-bottle and throwing away the rifle. Helpless, I stood and witnessed one of the thousands of tragedies that have occurred in those dark fastnesses.

Suddenly the elephant seized the boy by the neck, threw him into the air with a terrific jerk, and then smashed him down in front of him on the hard ground. Poor Juma lay motionless, and the elephant began smelling the corpse from head to foot. Next the great animal trampled the water-bottle into the ground. He then returned to the man, again smelt him, stamped on him with his fore-foot, then lifted him in his trunk and hurled him into the thicket. After which, still making curious noises, he moved towards the west. There I remained for the night in dire distress, uncomfortable and apprehensive because I had not been able to recover my rifle. In the morning I heard the boys shouting, and when they heard Juma had been killed they at once attributed his death to the killing of the snake.

On that particular safari I was away six months and arrived in Dar-es-Salaam with ivory worth £3600. The inhabitants became quite excited and talked a great deal about my bag. Several men gave notice to their employers, bought my rifles, and, taking my boys as guides, disappeared into the bush for three months. Six of them travelled to my hunting grounds, and during that time two of them died of fever and three had to be rescued by the Government. Only one man remained, and he did not meet with success. All suffered extreme hardships, since they were not able to obtain sufficient food, because they did not know the various articles of diet to be found in the veld.

CHAPTER ELEVEN

Jungle Ways of Man and Beast

ONE DOES NOT want to speak only of the excitements of the chase to make the blood run hot as that last split second brings one final loophole for escape from disaster. Personally— though I have enjoyed the dangerous hours, and relive them with, I hope, forgivable gusto as we yarn here — to me the ways of men, beasts, and birds have unending attraction.

I used to watch the natives on the Rufiji at their fishing. They always took with them their medicine man, whose duty it was to protect them from crocodiles. When they were approaching a fishing region fifty men went into the water and kept up a perpetual din and splashing in order to send the cowardly crocodile into hiding. Should one of the saurians be located at the bottom of the pool by the feet of the natives the medicine man went along, the noise was intensified, and the witch-doctor dived, seized the crocodile, and dispatched it with a spear. The natives believed that this saurian-killing power of the medicine man was a special ability, but this is not so; for when a great deal of noise is created a crocodile will always creep into a hole in the river-banks and lie so still as to appear dead. You may then hit it and strike it as much as you desire, but it will not move. The crocodile generally grabs one lonely victim, and finishes him off by drowning.

Crocodiles lay their soft-shelled eggs in the winter season, when the floods have subsided. They then come out on to the sand-banks, dig a hole with their tails, and scatter sand in all directions. They proceed to lay their eggs in layers, covering each layer with sand, and I have found as many as sixty eggs in one nest. It is a quaint sight to witness baby crocodiles emerging from the shells, lifting their heads, then sniffing, and next making a bee-line for the nearest water.

The crocodile is capable of killing a full-grown rhinoceros. It will lie in waiting, and when an animal comes to drink seizes it by the foot or nose. A rhino caught in this manner will lower its head and try to free itself by the use of its horns — tactics all in favor of the crocodile, who moves deeper into the water. Then it tightens its grip, and the victim is speedily drowned. If the animal resisted by backing away from the water it could, in most instances, get the best of the fight; but if the beast moves forward it is lost, and I am satisfied that even a young elephant can be defeated in this manner, although I have never actually witnessed an encounter between a crocodile and an elephant. I can declare, however, that elephants evidently regard crocodiles as their enemies, for whenever they drink where crocodiles are in the vicinity they hit the water with their trunks. I have also noticed that the adult elephants drink first, as though to reconnoitre the water for foes.

There are many nature stories concerning the crocodile. One is that birds take the food from between his teeth when he is asleep. I am of the opinion that the bird actually cleans the edges of the jaws from water lice and such-like parasites. I have seen fish performing the same services for the hippo. My reason for saying this is that the serrated teeth of a crocodile are set far apart and are always beautifully clean, for it does not chew. On one occasion, after killing a crocodile, my boys cut the reptile open, and we found the intact body of a small baboon in his belly. A crocodile's stomach is frequently full of stones and pebbles, always smooth, and generally white. The process of digestion takes place in the stomach through the medium of the grinding of the stones.

Away from water the crocodile is extremely agile, and moves so quickly that no man could catch it; it does not fight, and its sole object is to escape. One day during the dry season, while proceeding along a sandy river-bed, my dogs began barking and dashed off to an ant-bear hole. They were too terrified to enter, so my boys got a large stick and began poking in the hole. We expected to flush a leopard, but to our surprise, a crocodile emerged.

While on this subject of water-loving animals I might mention that I have found hippo thirty miles inland during the dry season. On the other hand, off Cape Delgado, in Portuguese East Africa, there were hippo five miles out from shore. I also have seen sharks and swordfish sixty miles upstream in a river.

Some natives declare that the elephant will take a crocodile out of the water, carry it some distance, split the fork of a tree, wedge the crocodile inside, and leave it. This is an absurd piece of fiction, but I do know that a full-grown elephant will seize a crocodile in shallow water, drag it out, and trample it to pieces. Most animals, it seems, like man, loathe crocodiles, but the hippo and crocodile are not enemies, and it is quite a common sight to view them lying together on the sand-banks.

Methods of angling on the Zambesi would have made no appeal to Izaak Walton. One, for instance, was to take seed-pods of the mimosa, break them into a basket, and lower it into a still pool four or five feet deep. The seeds have a peculiar effect on the fish, for in a very short time they float dazed on the surface, and are very easily caught. An hour afterwards those remaining in the pool become perfectly normal and swim away.

One particular kind of fish in the Zambesi is the electric fish; in appearance it is similar to the barbel, with smooth skin but spotted slightly with brown and yellow markings, the biggest being twelve to fourteen inches long. A fish of this size could not possibly be held in the hands, for the shock from it is so great that the moment one touched it the arm would be contracted with violent cramp. I experimented with these fish in order to study their reactions. If they lay quite still on the ground one could touch them without result, but the moment they showed resistance great care was needed, as the movement had the effect of generating a powerful electric current. The natives themselves knew this, and before emptying the nets they would set light to a grass torch, and with the aid of pointed sticks discard all the electric fish, which they never eat.

Another aspect of wild life in Africa which has always engaged my close attention relates to the simian family. Along the Rufiji the natives ate baboons, and also grey monkeys. They hunted the baboon with so much zeal that in two nights they would exterminate a whole troop. Their method of hunting was to use nets made from the bark of a baobab-tree; the rope used for the mesh was about one-eighth to a quarter of an inch thick, while the net itself was about ten yards in length. Every four feet small stacks of hard wood were fastened to the net, and in the case of a well-organized baboon hunt, as many as fifty nets would be employed at night while the baboons were sleeping. The natives placed their nets firmly in the ground by means of stakes. The hunters remained in hiding until daybreak, when they walked towards the baboons, who, becoming alarmed, jumped to the ground and ran into the traps, and soon became so entangled that they could not move. The natives then rushed up and speared them. In all the parts where these nets were used the baboon is practically exterminated.

They are most destructive creatures. They live in high kloofs and inaccessible crags, and can clamber along the precipitous sides of cliffs like spiders. Leopards greatly relish a feed of baboon, and are present in large numbers wherever baboons dwell. The spotted cats do not, however, seek hostilities with baboons in troops; they prefer to ambush one that is solitary, or young. I have witnessed more than one fight between leopard and baboon, and would invariably put my money on the big monkey. A baboon's eye-teeth are a full inch and a half long and extremely sharp. They do not bite as a dog does, but rush at the quarry, get it firmly with the two hands, turn the victim over, and plunge their teeth into the jugular vein.

When hunting for food baboons travel from one stone to another, roll the stone over, and kill whatever they find, scorpions and spiders being specially favored tit-bits. The baboon kills a scorpion by giving it a few taps with its hands to make the creature stop wriggling; it then attacks its tail, removes the poisonous sting, and eats it alive.

On the Rovuma river there was a bag baboon that had become a man-eater. Just where the river enters the sea on the east coast there is a swamp six miles wide covered with mangrove-trees and encircled by a footpath, along which the natives travel from one side of the morass to the other. Here this ferocious baboon had taken up its quarters, and when an isolated native came past it would attack and tear open the stomach of its victim. It would then break the skull, tear out the brains, which it devoured, and leave the rest of the body. The natives were unable to catch it, and were so terrified of the brute that eventually they left their village.

Leopards sometimes become man-eaters. These spotted cats are as silent as the grave, and will creep through holes and entrances to a hut, where they will snatch a victim and run. A lion will attempt to break down the door, whereas a leopard will silently dig a hole between the mud and poles, and slink in. I therefore consider a leopard that has gone man-eater a most formidable foe. I cannot say why they become man-eaters, for I have never killed a leopard suffering from poisoning by porcupine quills.

A leopard is one of the hardest animals to shoot, on account of its wariness and extreme agility. In the day-time it climbs on to a projecting branch of a tree, and selects a well-chosen outlook. It sights you before you see it, and when it becomes a man-eater it is a most dangerous beast. It remains invisible, and an unwary traveller passing below its vantage-point is immediately pounced on. It kills an animal by getting under the neck, into which its claws are deeply dug, and then it chokes its victim. I have seen many sheep, goats, young cattle, and buck killed by leopards, but never with their necks broken. Marks of teeth on the throat and an unbroken neck are sure signs that a leopard has been the aggressor.

By experience and observation the hunter soon learns to know what species of animal has killed. If the marks are on top of the neck it is the kill of a lion; signs of attack in the ribs denote the work of a hyena, which bites through the thinner flesh over the ribs and tears out the entrails; the wild dog commences gnawing the soft flesh at the back of the leg, and, as I have already explained, eats as he pursues, weakening the animal through loss of blood.

The best place to hunt for leopards is near the water, and the most suitable times are very early in the morning and in the later afternoon, when they are wandering along the banks. Like most beasts, leopards have their own particular lairs, and only wild dogs will drive them to seek new haunts. The wild dog is their hereditary enemy, and if leopards could not climb into trees for safety they would be killed in every encounter with these ferocious creatures.

I must add one or two peculiarities of elephants, since I have studied them more than any other of African big game — often at far too close quarters! The belief that they have a common burial ground is sheer romance. I have picked up at least five hundred pounds' worth of ivory from dead animals scattered in various parts of Africa. The only excuse for the myth is that dead elephants are naturally more often found in the densest parts of thickets, for it is the instinct of all animals to retreat to solitude when they die. When an elephant feels the pangs of death it will go where there is water, and where it will be undisturbed, there to remain until the end comes.

Here's another "hunter's tale." Often it has been contended that these pachyderms help each other to escape if they are wounded. I have never witnessed an instance of this. When disturbed elephants will run in the same manner as a flock of stampeding sheep. They then close in on one another, and if a wounded beast happens to be in the middle it may involuntarily be supported by the others until it drops out, but this does not imply that its companions are deliberately helping it to get away. If, in such circumstances, there are young ones with the herd, the elephants will often put the young in front, and will not allow them to get behind, but this trait is a habit with all wild animals.

Another interesting point: the elephant will visit its dead with almost a human sense of bereavement. In Portuguese Nyasaland there is a region of thick bush — said to be almost impenetrable, for it is sixty miles in length and thirty miles in width — and in the whole length and breadth there are only two known water-holes. When the rainy season set in I often entered this thicket as far as I could, penetrating sometimes as much as twenty miles, and finding water-holes dug by the elephants to catch the rain water. One morning I entered this no-man's land in pursuit of what the natives had nicknamed the "Iron Herd." They declared that there were enormous bulls among them, and said that no hunter had ever been able to shoot one. The herd numbered fully two hundred, and the moment the beasts got scent of danger they would trumpet and charge in the direction of the scent.

I decided to see whether these stories were true, and so, very early one morning, we started off in search. My boys and I all took water-bottles, but the heat was intense that by midday none of us had a drop left. From the track it was clear that the

beasts were within close distance, and I was therefore determined to continue the pursuit. About two o'clock we saw them,
scattered over an area of five hundred yards, the majority
standing and sleeping. The wind was in our favor, and we got
in among them, sometimes passing within a few paces of cows,
calves, and young bulls. Of these I took no notice, for I was in
quest of big bulls, who are easy to locate because of the loud
rumblings of the stomach and the flapping of their ears.

Right ahead of us we could hear one, and we proceeded
silently and carefully until we came to a large baobab-tree.
The elephant was under its shade, and I tip-toed to the other
side of the tree, but found he was standing in such a position
that I could not fire an effective shot. I therefore waited, for
while an elephant stands and sleeps he moves from one foot to
the other to relieve the great weight of his body, and I
expected he would change to a position more advantageous
to me. But he did not shift his stance, and I waited so long that
some of the elephants we had passed started moving, and the
trampling of bush could be heard in all directions. This
endangered our position, because of the likelihood of some of
the others getting our wind. I therefore had to take a chance,
fired, and got my bull right between the shoulders, a shot that
I knew would kill him, although he might travel some distance
before dropping. The rest began trumpeting, and rushed
away. We took cover behind the trunk of the baobab-tree,
which was fully eight feet in diameter, and the herd passed us
like an express train.

We had to leave their spoor to search for water, and were
lucky before nightfall in finding a muddy drinking-hole the
animals used. Next morning at sunrise we took up the spoor
of one, and within a quarter of an hour were able to guess how
far he had gone. If an elephant is hovering around near at hand
he moves in circles, but if the spoor is in a bee-line you may
sometimes have to follow it for fifty miles. This animal was

heading in a direct line for the north, but after we had followed the spoor for five miles we found that it had suddenly changed its direction due east. Two miles farther on we came to a heap of dried bones lying in an open clearing — the remnants of the skeleton of an elephant. The tracks went right up to the skeleton and plainly told the story; the bull had loitered there at least half an hour, for he visited practically every one of the scattered bones. The spoor then deviated in the northerly direction, which showed that he had gone out of his way for at least two miles to visit the place of the dead. I have observed several similar instances where elephants have gone miles out of their paths to visit the final resting-place of an ancestor — or, perhaps, a spouse.

How near the jungle beasts are some of the jungle men! Before the Belgian Government made a determined effort to stamp out cannibalism any native of another tribe was liable to be caught and killed by hunting parties of man-eaters. The individual who had actually done the killing was entitled to the fingers and toes, which he cut off and ate raw. At one time I was in close contact with one of these tribes, and saw them eating human flesh. They explained to me their gruesome methods of preparing a meal, and stated that after the body had been soaked in hot water the skin was scraped off. In the centre of the village a pit was dug in the ground about two feet deep and long enough to contain the victim. A large fire was made in this pit, and was left burning throughout the day. Meanwhile the body was stuffed with plantains, and in the evening the fire was scraped out and the pit was lined with plantain-leaves. The body was next laid on top of these, and more plantain-leaves were added. The ashes from the fire were then used to cover the pit, the body being left there for the remainder of the night. In the morning the horrible feast began.

Distinctly grim, but part of the story of the jungles.

Jungle Man

On Lake Tanganyika there lived a cannibal and his wife, who had escaped from Belgian territory, and one day it was discovered that the wife had disappeared. The people of the village made inquiries, and the husband was arrested. In court he affirmed that he had not been able to resist the temptation to taste human flesh again as he did not get enough meat, and eventually he had been forced to kill and eat his wife.

I was also present at the hearing of a case, as late as the beginning of 1914, in a Portuguese fort named Mtarika, on the Lujenda river, in Nyasaland. Local natives laid a complaint against a certain cannibal living in their village who, they declared, removed the bodies of their dead after they were buried. Investigation revealed in this man's hut a number of human arms and legs which had been cured and smoked over a fire. The flesh-eater excused himself on the ground that he had not killed anyone, but had only taken the bodies after they had been buried !

CHAPTER TWELVE

Thirst

THE DOCTORS told me it was time I had a holiday; Africa had taken its toll on my health. So I made a trip to Europe; and I guess the months I enjoyed most were those I spent on the way back with the Bedouins. I liked their nomadic ways, and they treated me as a brother. We swapped hunting yarns.

Another feature of the journey was that in Jerusalem I met the girl who afterwards became my wife. Alas, that idyll was short-lived. Not long after she had come out to the Rufiji to marry me Africa claimed her.

I mention my marriage because there is this fact concerning it which falls into the narrative of my journeyings. I decided to be the first farmer on the Rufiji — growing cotton — and secured an area for this purpose. There I built a home for my bride-to-be, a handsome two-storied house beside the river, and I named it "Tindwa." Nearly all my money was expended on the place, and when this was completed, and the hunting season opened, I installed a German foreman, and returned to the bush to hunt elephants. Now, here is a sample of the way the German mind can work, showing that the arrogant attitude adopted towards all other races is no new thing of a Hitler régime; it is bred in the national character.

During my absence in Palestine the German settlers pestered the Government to refuse foreigners entrance into the country, and prevent them from making money by hunting — my own case in particular was cited. It was sheer jealousy, for the Germans themselves had tried the game, lost a number of lives, and acomplished little. Although every pfennig of the money I made was put into the farm, the authorities made their hunting laws as difficult as they could for me, and in the course of time I was forced to go to the Belgian Congo and Portuguese Nyasaland, which, of course, involved a great deal of additional expense.

Then, suddenly, without deigning to offer a reason, the Government refused me a license, and I received a private letter saying that shooting was *verboten* to me. At the same time the Government continued to issue licenses wholesale to Germans, and even gave their own nationals permission to shoot on my farm! Two German hunters who came to Tindwa were brothers named Ringler, and they were more successful than their predecessors. They obtained the services of my old boys and guides, who took them to the elephant country, pointed out the best animals, and helped them to slay a dozen large tuskers.

But it so happened that one morning the brothers went in different directions after elephant. The elder followed a spoor for four hours, when he came to a bull, which he wounded. He and his boys went in pursuit of the beast for the best part of the afternoon, until they were forced to leave the chase and return to camp. Next day both Ringlers set out, and followed the tracks until they came to very dense bush into which the elephant had entered. The hunters were proceeding slowly and silently, when suddenly one of the boys whispered that the bull was lying dead. The elder brother instinctively quickened his pace, thinking the bull was the one he had wounded the day before. He had his hands ready to measure the tusks when suddenly the elephant rose and trampled him to death.

Here is a case in point showing the foolishness of believing different, though dogmatic, hunting stories, such as the one to the effect that the elephant never lies down to sleep. I had shot over two hundred elephants before I observed that they sometimes do lie down to sleep. One morning, after following a wounded bull which had gone into the bush, a boy pointed out the elephant lying down and perfectly still. As in Ringler's case, the spoor led me to where he was lying, with legs outstretched, like a gigantic horse. I walked towards the animal and then saw three elephants lying down. I knew I had not killed the trio, but before I could even fire they got our wind, jumped up, and ran away.

Two other Germans, representing the famous zoo and menagerie firm of Hagenbeck, came to camp on my farm, and one morning both of them set out in quest of elephant. Towards noon they came back marching along the river-bank, where the grass in places was ten feet high and extremely thick. Here they came on buffalo spoor, which they followed, and unexpectedly came upon a bull. The buffalo charged, and although the Hagenbeck hunters fired two shots the buffalo gored one of them to death. It is always foolhardy for all but the most experienced hunters to follow a buffalo into reeds or thick bush, for a buffalo can see and hear the movements of the grass. They are clever enough to know that their best method of attack is to waylay an enemy at close quarters. In more open country they seldom attack, and will run for cover.

While I was on my farm four Germans lost their lives through elephants, and one was killed by a lion. One of the more terrible episodes was the tragedy that happened to the captain of the *Tormondo*, a little river steamer. Twice a month he came up-stream with supplies. The steamer travelled only during the day, on account of sand-banks, and on this occasion the captain tied up at a place of anchorage early in the afternoon. As was his habit, he left the steamer to proceed seven miles inland to a military outpost, named Mahoro, where he played cards. He did not leave for his ship until midnight.

The police lent the skipper a mule, and were alarmed when, in the early hours of the morning, the beast stampeded into the camp riderless. They sent natives out immediately, and after they had gone about two miles the boys heard lions grunting in front of them. With their hurricane lamps they moved cautiously in the direction of the sound, and discovered the lions ten yards off the road in tall grass. They saw human remains in the middle of the road, and when the police were fetched they could scarcely identify what was left of the mutilated skipper. The lions of the Rufiji had claimed another victim!

There are dangers lurking in the "Dark Continent" other, and sometimes more deadly, than wild man or beast, and the greatest of these is thirst. In equatorial Africa the heat is often so intense that one's drinking capacity is unbelievably great, and, in like ratio, the torment that follows lack of water is unbearable. On several of my safaris lives were lost from thirst, but the worst experience I ever had in this respect was in 1913, while I was hunting elephants in Portuguese Nyasaland.

My headquarters were established at a Portuguese fort, named Mtarika, situated on the wide reaches of the Lujenda river. Mtarika was the name of the Paramount Chief of the district, where there was excellent elephant-hunting; and here I shot a number of good tuskers. The chief told me that two days away was an old village in the vicinity of which were even bigger bulls than were to be found in his district. Mtarika's people informed me that they had deserted the village ten years previously, and that good drinking-water was to be found there in abundance by digging in the sand of a dry river-bed.

The distance tó the village was fifty miles, and the intervening country was covered with dense scrub bush and sporadic forests of small bamboo — an extremely trying country in which to travel. My boys obtained calabashes in which to carry water, and, in addition, I had a number of canvas bags and a few aluminum water-bottles. In this bush the heat was terrific, and we had only gone a few miles before we were attacking the water-supplies. The morning after we left Mtarika we broke camp very early, and the guide said that we should reach water about four o'clock in the afternoon.

We set off at a good gait — thirsty work. By midday our water was finished, and very soon our throats were parched. In other climates, such as humid England, a few hours' abstinence from water is unnoticed, but where we were it was not long before one could not swallow and every breath seemed a burn. By mid-afternoon, under the torrid sun, four of the boys were unable to continue. I told them to lie down under a bush, and encouraged them by saying that I could see large green trees which outlined a river in the near distance. The lips of all my boys looked as if they had been whitewashed with lime. We pushed on towards the water in silence, for no one spoke, since, under such circumstances, it is wiser to conserve the saliva.

We reached the river at sunset, and, to my dismay, the guides began to ask one another where they had obtained water in former years. One pointed out a sycamore-tree, saying that there he had found water, while another pointed to a second sycamore-tree and declared: "That is the place." But there was not a sign of water anywhere, and in a torment of thirst we began to dig in the sand under one of the big wild fig-trees which lined the course of the dry river-bed.

Matters were serious. I dispatched two guides to the east and two to the west to search for the fluid, upon the discovery of which our very lives depended. In the meantime I and the remainder continued digging with almost frantic haste in the sand with our hands. At a depth of four feet our hands encountered damp sand, but to delve farther was very difficult, for we had no spades, and when we chucked up the sand the walls of the pit kept caving in. We kept on, perspiration bathing us, thirst ever increasing. We got down to six feet, and there found so much moisture that the boys took handfuls of the sand and stuffed it into their mouths, just for the gratifying taste of dampness. Then to our disgust, we encountered a big, flat rock which seemed to fill the whole river-bed. There was nothing for it but to cut our losses (of time) and, discarding all hope of immediate relief, make tracks back to the Lujenda river.

"Throw away everything," I told the boys. "It's each man for himself."

Contrary to general belief, natives are not adepts at finding their way through dense bush, and I therefore warned them to keep up with me, stating that I would not answer any shouting if any person got lost during the night. I'll tell you why. Perhaps you have heard of tablets, pebbles, and stones which preserve moisture in the mouth; but such devices are useless in cases of dire plight such as that in which we had now found ourselves. From years of experience I have found that the only effective method of retaining the moisture in the mouth is not to speak at all, but to grind one's teeth together and keep the tongue absolutely still. When a person is very thirsty there is a natural tendency to move the tongue round the mouth and swallow continuously, and this is the worst possible thing to do. If a person keeps his tongue behind the teeth the mouth will retain the moisture much longer than if the tongue is moving.

Well, we started off, and I made a bee-line for the four men who had surrendered to the *force majeure* of circumstances that afternoon, and found them in much better condition than when in the hot sun. I explained our failure to the boys, and told them I was going to walk fast and that they must try to keep up with me or otherwise they would be lost for good. Just before midnight the weak ones began to fall out, one after the other; we were then travelling through scrub bamboo almost as dense as grass, and walking was terribly difficult, for

152

we had always to keep our hands in front and brush the bamboos out of the way. The natives next started calling and shouting, and, in spite of my warning that I would not answer their calls, I did so to get the desperate safari together again. But after a time, since they still cried out, I decided not to reply to any more calls, but to make a bee-line for the nearest point to the river. For I was feeling pretty well done. Through torturing hours I marched, and when it grew light I saw that only seven boys of my fourteen were left with me. By ten o'clock only three natives were still in sight. Although we could see the outline of the trees bordering the banks of the Lujenda, the river was still miles away, and we were becoming so weak that I doubted if we would ever reach water.

When the sun was overhead by good fortune we came to fresh elephant spoor, and in desperation I decided to follow the tracks — planning to shoot an animal in order to obtain water from its belly. After I had tracked the elephant spoor for two miles we emerged from the bamboos into parkland country, wherein the trees were high, quite clear of undergrowth, and we could see for a distance of two hundred yards ahead of us. The twigs and leaves dropped by the elephants told me that they were quite close, but the wind was bad. The only thing to do, however, was to continue on the spoor and hope for the best. Five hundred yards farther on I suddenly saw two or three elephants of monstrous size. I quickened my pace, but immediately I did so the elephants got my wind, lifted up their trunks, and stuck their ears out — always a sign of alarm. Then they started to run. I was so weak and overcome with thirst that I could not run, but I struggled forward in a frantic endeavor to try to shoot one of them. I had to fire at the last one of the group, and felt a wave of joy run through me as I saw him fall. But he got up almost immediately. Three times in succession I dropped the elephant, and the fourth time, when

I was more or less broadside on to him, I gave him another bullet through the ear and finished him off. We staggered to the carcase.

I indicated to one boy where to cut in order to obtain the water of the elephant, the reservoir being under the last rib. The boy put the knife in clumsily, although I had warned him to cut carefully. He burst the elephant's water-bag and hacked into the entrails, and a spout of water and blood, about an inch thick, shot out of the beast's stomach.

My boys were Mohammedans, and their law prohibited them from eating the flesh of an animal unless the throat had been cut by one of the faithful, but discipline went to the winds now, so excited and tormented were they. They struggled forward to drink the mixture as it shot out. I must confess that I too did not think I could live another ten minutes without water, yet I flinched from that drink. One of the boys had an old tin and also a calabash, so I poured some of the unpalatable mixture into the calabash and strained it through my handkerchief into a tin. Then I drank it, and, although it had a bitter taste from the blood, water, and the different herbs the elephant had eaten, it was wonderfully refreshing. The foul liquid undoubtedly saved our lives, but while it quenched our burning thirst for a time, ten minutes later we were again tormented.

Only three men were left out of the fourteen who had started with me, and I told them to fill the calabash, go back on our trail, and try to find some of the men who had fallen out during the night. This they did, and about three o'clock in the afternoon they returned with four of the others. Had we not sent water back there would have been but four survivors, for when the rescuers found the quartette only one was still sitting up against the tree. He had carefully covered the other three with long grass as a form of burial rite, and had propped himself up stoically awaiting death.

Thirst

I am sure that if it had not been for the liquid provided by the elephant not one of us would have lived, and had we died in that waterless country, utterly devoid of any landmarks, our bodies would never have been discovered. There was plenty of the foul beverage, and as we were completely exhausted I decided to stay by the elephant's carcase until the next day. Here I found another way of drinking elephant water. One of the boys had a little ground corn with him, and so we mixed this with the water, which give it a floury taste, and was certainly preferable to the natural fluid.

For food we roasted the flesh of the animal. The most edible and tasty part of the elephant is the heart, which I estimate weighs at least twenty pounds. An elephant's heart is similar to that of a sheep, and the upper portion of it is covered with fat. We cut the heart with a sharp stick into small pieces, then took a portion of the heart, next a piece of fat, again a piece of heart, and so, placing the chunks in a row on a stick, roasted them in the flames, and obtained a really tasty dish.

During the night we cut out the tusks, and the next morning we started off again on our way to the Lujenda river. After we had been travelling through very high trees a honey-bird came twittering to us. We followed the bird down a kloof, in which there was a big donga full of wild fig-trees, where the bird led us to a beehive, and we secured the honey.

"The trees are green, so there must be water close by," I pointed out to the boys, and, surely enough, we came to a beautiful spring with crystal-clear water that bubbled out of the ground under some rocks, ran about twenty yards, and then disappeared underground again. It was heaven. We threw away the water from the elephant, and camped there for the rest of the day, reaching Mtarika the following afternoon, where I stayed inside the fort with the Portuguese Commandant. It had been reported to the Paramount Chief that seven men had died of thirst, and the next morning we were informed that the Paramount Chief had arrived with a very big impi of natives, that he required compensation for the seven dead men, and that unless the award was forthcoming he would make war.

After a long consultation with the chief and the Portuguese Commandant we came to a settlement, in the terms of which the chief agreed to supply men to accompany the survivors of my ill-fated expedition in an endeavor to find the dead bodies, and prove that the men had died from thirst and were not killed. The chief was actually accusing me of murder.

This portion of Portuguese Nyasaland had never been conquered, and we were in grave danger of being attacked and overwhelmed. The search party duly set forth with a good supply of water, and declared that they would be back on the third day. It was not until late on the fourth day that two of the party turned up with the news that they could not find the bodies, and that they themselves lost three men from thirst. This finished the argument with the Paramount Chief. I emphasized that it was not on my suggestion that we had gone on the expedition, but that he himself had recommended the country, and had said there was plenty of water to be found. With these arguments and a tactful gift of presents we settled the dispute, and it was admitted that the calamity which had befallen the chief's people was no fault of mine.

I have had some rough treks in my time, but that nightmare journey through the terrible thirst-land of Porutguese East Africa was one of the worst of all my journeyings.

CHAPTER THIRTEEN

The Way of a Hun

ONE THING about the German — his faults are forthright. His are the sins of a bully.

I have already recorded how he autocratically withdrew my license to shoot, just because I succeeded where he couldn't — for the bully is ever a bad loser — but that was almost trivial compared with the high-handed manner in which he coolly stole my farm from me. I had no redress — except the one I took, as I shall describe — but I am convinced no other race in the world would have acted officially as the authorities in German East Africa did. The German thinks that whatever he does is proved right by his power to do it. His is the law of the jungle, which knows no morals, only might.

I was up in Portuguese Nyasaland at the time. Captain Hemming and I had gone because the Germans had withdrawn our licenses; up there we were free. It was wild, unsubdued country, and, though nominally under Portuguese rule, was actually so savage that when we asked the authorities for permission to shoot they made us sign a document to the effect that should ill befall us we alone were to blame and no responsibility rested on them.

When we had penetrated the country, the first white men to establish relations with some of the tribes, those same Portuguese authorities didn't mind asking me to guide an expedition against the Paramount Chief of one large area, whose name was Mtaka. They had been after him for about four years, previously, but the wily chief had ambushed that expedition, and only one man, named Da Conia, escaped, by eluding his pursuers in the jungle. It was when this little war was over — for I agreed to lead the punitive expedition because Mtaka's country gave refuge to all the outlaws from Central Africa, German East Africa, and Portuguese territories — that I received a letter from the authorities in German East Africa advising me to sell my farm on the Rufiji to a German officer — one Hauptmann Blake. They stated that Blake was prepared to pay four hundred pounds for my farm — an utterly absurd price, as the house alone had cost me more than double that price. In addition, I had done a great deal of clearing, for the bush was very dense, and the usual price paid for clearing trees in German East Africa was ten pounds per morgen.[1]

They stated that if I refused to sell to Blake they would confiscate the farm and give it to him. I took this as a challenge from the Government, and replied that I was not prepared to sell to anyone, and should they confiscate it I would revenge myself by shooting elephants in their territory, without a license, until I had secured the full value of the property.

I sent the letter by native runner, and within a month received the astonishing reply that my farm had been given to Hauptmann Blake, and that I had no further claim to it. That's the Hun's way — take what you want if there's no one to stop you.

Captain Hemming read these letters, and had been present on my farm about three years previously when Blake passed through and had been very anxious to buy the property. I was not in residence at the time, but Blake told Hemming that he was going to commence farming there, and if he could not obtain my property he would not look at any other. It was perfectly clear that this confiscation had been an organized conspiracy between Blake and the Government. I wrote a letter to Newala, informing the Germans there that from then

---

[1] Two and a quarter acres.

onward I should be hunting elephants in the district, and I challenged them to catch me.

I set about the business almost immediately. Since Hemming decided he would not poach in German territory I took with me a man named Mare, who had wandered into our camp without any equipment, one of the world's gipsies.

We left camp on the south bank of the flooded Rovuma during the rainy season, and crossed over to German East Africa. Marching along the main road, which ran through very bad bush, we arrived at a spot within three miles of the German police outpost, called Sassawarra. Up to this point we had seen plenty of spoor, and we now left the road and struck across country towards the east, following the promising tracks of a herd of tuskers. It was a novel experience for Mare, who never before had been after elephants.

Two miles on we came upon the rear of the herd. Although there was a large number of elephants standing within ten paces of us, I did not consider it advisable to leave the spoor of the bulls. Thus we had to pass between a number of elephants, and Mare became excited. I was in front and had fully observed the elephants on either side, but I knew that the ones I wanted were ahead. Mare, thinking I had not seen the herd, would tug at my coat every now and then, and very excitedly point out that we were passing elephants; I had all my work cut out to keep him quiet.

When eventually I came up to the bull I had been tracking I got broadside on to him, shot him in the ear, and he dropped like a stone. As the elephants we had passed heard the shot they came tearing through the bush in our direction. Mare rushed to one side, almost ran into an elephant, and came racing back with a bewildered look on his face.

Some of the elephants, trumpeting loudly, passed within four paces of where we stood. There were none worth shooting, and I stood ready with my .475 in case of attack, but fortunately there was no occasion to fire, and the herd disappeared into the bush. This shot was fired within four miles of the police camp, and I knew perfectly well that they had heard us, and would be after us before long, for I had told the native chief when we crossed the river that he could inform the Germans that I was bent on shooting their elephants.

After the tusks had been cut out we travelled during the afternoon and reached a spruit, where we found water. We slept there, and next morning, following the spoor of a number of bulls, overtook the herd, of which I shot three. There were no exciting incidents in this case, and as we had eight tusks, each of which was a good load for the boys, we returned to camp.

Round number one.

When we arrived at camp and Hemming saw the magnificent tusks I had obtained he changed his mind and said he would like to accompany me to Deutsche Ost Afrika, so after two days we all started off. We recrossed the Rovuma, and went to a native village in German territory, where they told me that the Germans were after me, and that I would have to be most careful. We stayed that night just outside a village in the bush. The natives said elephants were to be found in their lands throughout the night, and that they fed until seven o'clock in the morning.

The next day, guided by a villager, we set off, and had only gone half a mile when we reached the kaffir-corn fields, where we found that a herd of elephants had just vacated the place. We followed them along the river-banks through dangerously high elephant grass, reeds, and very dense bush, where it was impossible to see an elephant if he was standing still until within four or five paces of it.

We proceeded cautiously, and eventually came to a sharp bend in the river where the banks were several feet high. Just as we reached the middle of the curve we heard elephants

"Thus I collected the cost of my farm" (see p. 168)

"They were exceedingly proud of their bag" (see p. 215)

charging. They were on the bend, and as we were in the open they had come out of the bush to get at us. As they charged I shot four of them, one of them being within four paces of me. Hemming also bagged one, so that we had plenty of work for the rest of the day in cutting out the tusks. All the natives from the village — men, women, and children — came to live for the time being where the elephants lay, erected temporary huts, and gorged themselves on meat.

We learned later that shortly after we had vacated this camp the German police arrived and arrested the whole bunch of natives for shooting the elephants. The aborigines had the fright of their lives, but were released when they told the Germans that it was I who had shot the beasts.

As we now had ten tusks to carry we decided to return to the camp, and did so — crossing through a broken terrain which consisted of small kopjes, bush, and rocks of blue granite, some of which were the size of an elephant, and were, indeed, several times mistaken by us for the beasts. We came to the end of the scattered bush, and were just about to enter another jungle, which was about a hundred yards in front of us, when I told Hemming I was sure that what he saw were elephants, not rocks. Suddenly one of the "rocks" lifted its trunk and began to flap its ears!

I immediately told the porters to sit down, and Hemming and I ran towards the animals, which were standing in the open in the sun. One side of the clearing consisted of a bamboo forest, and the elephants were standing in the corner where this forest joined the other clump of bush. We had to search for the bulls, and eventually I saw that they were standing behind the herd, against the bamboos. Once again we had to pass the larger part of the herd in order to be able to fire at the bulls. I got in the first shot, and dropped the biggest. When the herd stampeded Hemming turned and ran in a southerly direction for all he was worth, for he carried only a

small-bore rifle, while I stood firing until I had dropped four
more bulls, and then, as my cartridges were finished and my
ammunition boy had cleared off, I stood still while the elephants tore past me, trumpeting loudly. When the larger
portion had passed I ran as fast as I could northward to escape
the remainder, which were also coming in my direction. I shall
never forget the next few moments. I stepped on a bamboo
that was lying on the ground, slipped, and fell on the broad
of my back, right in front of some of the oncoming monsters,
but, luckily, they turned and followed the rest.

Here again we were kept busy cutting the tusks out. Every
one set to work, and by the evening we had completed the
task. As we now had twenty tusks we decided to return to the
camp, and arrived back quite safely, although the German
police of the district were hot on our trail.

Round number two.

We stayed in camp for two days, and then I told Hemming
I was going back for what I hoped would be the last time.
Hemming said he was tired and would prefer to remain in
camp. Mare and I set off again. The river was in full flood,
and at least seven hundred yards broad, so we obtained a dug-
out from the natives on the Portuguese side, and crossed in
the evening. I had asked Hemming to send the dug-out to
meet us, on the eighth day, at a little spruit that flowed into
the Rovuma, the paddlers to remain there until we arrived.

On the first day we did not find any elephants worth shooting, but on the second, when we came up to them, I saw there
were some very large bulls among the herd. Of these I managed to shoot three. Elephants, I am certain, have some tele-
pathic method of communicating with one another, and after
one has been shooting in one particular district for about a
fortnight it is found that they suddenly seem to disappear
from that area, and travel in a straight line for another. This is
not confined to a single elephant or even to two or three herds;

herd after herd treks away in the same direction, which means they are leaving the district for some time, if not for good. It is only when it is observed that elephants zigzag across the country that one can be sure they are remaining there.

We travelled for several days looking for tuskers, but found none worth a shot, as all the big herds had trekked towards the north. On the eighth day, as our food-supply had almost come to an end, I started back for the Rovuma. The country, as I have said before, was very dense and terribly hot, there being hardly a breath of wind. Away from the big rivers not a drop of water was to be found, and we were getting into greater, and still greater, difficulties. Mare and all the natives were very ill, and early in the afternoon I realized that if we did not reach water before nightfall I should lose some of the men. I therefore climbed a high tree and looked over the countryside for signs of water. I noticed that the only likely spot was in quite a different direction from that in which we were travelling, but as it seemed to be only about five miles away I decided to reach it as soon as possible. About half-way to the place we came to a big vlei (marsh) covered with elephant tracks and grass. This was a sure sign that for some time elephants had been drinking there.

I stopped on the edge of the vlei, under a large tree, and told some of the boys to follow the elephant tracks into the grass and find water. Mare would not remain with me, and followed them. Five minutes later they returned and said there was no water in the vlei at all, but that there was only wet clay to be seen. All the natives, and Mare too, had actually been munching this clay in order to quench their thirst. They wanted to lie down there, but as I could see the outline of a river only about a mile away I encouraged them to get up and follow me. We reached the belt of green, and there found a beautifully clear stream of running water eight feet wide.

It is always dangerous to drink too much water when very

thirsty; but the moment the men saw the water they all rushed towards it, fell on their stomachs, and drank as fast as they could. I sat on the bank for a while to cool off, and warned them presently to stop drinking, otherwise they would all be ill. We were now exhausted, and as it was five o'clock in the afternoon we decided to remain here, famished, for the night.

During the dark hours a very large elephant passed within ten yards of us, but as an elephant makes no noise with his feet not one of us heard him, and it was only in the morning that I saw his tracks. This was the biggest elephant track I had seen since I commenced hunting in this district. I could put both my feet in his tracks, and then put four fingers in front of them before they reached the edge of the spoor. I decided immediately that we should have to get this fellow, and we followed the spoor down-stream. After we had tracked him for about seven miles I suddenly heard him rush away, from about ten paces in front of us, in the elephant grass. I climbed an ant-hill, and from this little summit observed the elephant at a distance of some two hundred yards. I fired behind the shoulders, and he ran for about ten yards, then raised his trunk and spouted blood into the air — a sure sign that he was dying. I gave him another shot through the ear, and he fell backward into the river-bed. His tusks penetrated the opposite bank into hard, compact soil for at least four feet. It was a long and difficult task to get those tusks out of the ground. Each weighed a hundred and eighty pounds, which meant that they were double loads. In the case of a double load I always got a stick about eight feet long and tied to it one tusk, which was then carried by two porters.

Every one was very hungry by now, and during the time the tusks were being removed meat was roasted over the fires, my whole safari enjoying a good meal. That night we slept in the bush again, and then proceeded to the place where we had to meet the boat. At night I sent the men to see if the canoe was there. They returned to say the boat was not there, but that there were marks showing the boys had arrived with the canoe, but instead of staying had returned to camp.

As we were now isolated we stayed there for a while, and then a honey-bird called us. Some of the boys followed it and found its nest in a tree. They cut it down with their axes, and while they were doing so about twenty local natives and a Jumbe, or head-man, arrived, drawn by the noise. The chief told me that all the German police of the district were on our track, and every chief had been given instructions to capture us.

None of these natives who knew me would make any attempt to catch me, for they regarded me as a friend who provided them with unlimited quantities of meat. We remained there for the rest of the day, and I learned that all the boats had been taken out of the river on the German side, and had been hidden away near a village which I knew. I explained to Mare that we should have to wait until evening, when we should stealthily proceed to this village where the chief had told us the canoes were.

After dark we stole along the bank, and when I got within fifty yards of the village we heard noises which indicated that there was a big gathering, probably a beer-drink in progress; so we stayed among the mealies for a while. I then told Mare that we would approach the gathering and demand a canoe. Mare and my natives pleaded with me not to do this, for they said there was a big jamboree in progress, and we might be overwhelmed.

While we were debating which course of action to take one of my boys stated that he knew of a crossing about three hours' march down the Rovuma, and practically opposite Hemming's camp. He said that although the river was very deep the water there would only reach up to our necks, even in flood-time. We decided to act on the boy's plan. It was pitch dark, and as I walked ahead I suddenly ran into a rope stretched across the path. I knew at once what it meant; it was a warning to every one that there was a lion trap within a few yards. This method of signalling danger is adopted throughout the country.

We had been told that two German police officers were in front of us, outspanned near the road, and practically opposite our camp, so we hurried, in order to avoid them, under cover of darkness. We had only gone a mile when in the improving light I suddenly saw a lion approaching me. I slipped the safety-catch on my rifle in case the lion attacked, but as soon as it saw me it stood still, and when I was within ten paces the beast walked off into the grass and stopped.

I did not say anything to Mare and the others, but marched on, while the lion remained until Mare passed, and then it let out a sudden grunt and Mare ran for his life. When he came up to me I reprimanded him for making so much noise, but could not help laughing when he indignantly replied: "You do not know that I was nearly killed by a lion."

I again warned him to walk softly with his number eleven boots and not to speak at all, as we were approaching the German camp. A mile farther we reached an opening in the bush, and there I saw two tents. Inside one of them the officers had a hurricane lamp over the table at which they had been sitting playing cards. We left the road, got into the elephant grass, and walked through it until we had left the camp far behind, when we took to the road again.

Five hundred yards farther along I saw a man approaching. He turned out to be an askari, and appeared very frightened. He told me that he was not anxious to interfere with us, but declared that these two officers and about ten askaris had been on our track from the first day after we had crossed the river on our previous trip. The askari also said that when I had shot the three elephants they had come up just afterwards, and had seen our camp-fire across the valley, but decided not to approach as they frankly funked doing so.

(During the First World War I actually captured one of these officers, and he corroborated the story told me by the askari.)

We were now only about three hundred yards from the deep ford of the river, so we told the askari that he could tell the Germans that we had recrossed the Rovuma into Portuguese territory, and that I did not intend to do any more shooting in their country as my farm was paid for. When we arrived at the river-bank I was wearing the usual kit — ordinary safari boots, puttees, khaki shorts which reached to my knees, and the long khaki shirt which was worn to hang over the shorts like a smock. I decided not to strip, for I knew that we should be able to obtain dry clothing at our camp.

The boy who knew the crossing walked in front of me, put a stick into the water, and found it was only about four feet deep. The river at this point must have been fully a thousand yards wide, and was running smoothly and quietly. Every one followed us into the water fully clothed. The river had a sandy bed without rocks, and we had gone about three hundred yards when we suddenly struck a strong current. The boy in front of me disappeared, and before I could stop myself I went down too, but Mare grabbed my hand, and I caught hold of the boy and hauled him to the surface.

We moved a little way up-stream until we found that we could turn and proceed in water that was between four and five feet deep. Then, with the bank only forty yards off, the boy in front slipped into a deep pool, and I followed him. The current was terrifically strong. When I came to the surface the boy who had fallen grabbed one of my legs, and I went down again. When I broke surface once more every one was struggling for his life. They had all caught hold of one another, and this naturally increased their precarious confusion. Not one had retained his load, so that all our ivory had gone to the bottom of the river.

It was a terrible spectacle, and I honestly thought that every one would be drowned, as the boys had lost their heads and were snatching at one another in panic. I was again submerged and then kicked myself free from the boy who was holding me, came to the surface, and swam towards the shore, where I seized a thick reed. As the boys passed me I threw out the reed, and one of them caught it. I pulled him towards the edge, and then secured another reed, and in this way all of them were pulled across to safety. Mare was in the centre of the boys, and when I got him out he lay down on the sand-bank gasping. He had swallowed so much water that he could hardly walk, and when I laughed at him he said to me in a sulky way, "Jy lag nog, maar my hoed is nog weg." ("You still laugh, but my hat is gone.") Hundreds of pounds of ivory had gone to the bottom of the river, but Mare was only concerned about his hat!

After a good night's rest every one was perfectly fit again, and the next morning I chose four of my best swimmers to salvage the ivory. The river was swarming with crocodiles, but as we made a lot of noise they did not come near us, and we recovered everything — with the exception of Mare's hat.

Round number three — but only just. . . .

Thus I collected the cost of my farm from the thieves.

CHAPTER FOURTEEN

Man-made Jungle

FROM THE jungle where wild things make eternal war — to the jungle of humanity, and the savagery of 1914.

Hemming and I were loafing on the Rovuma; after my incursions into German East Africa poaching ivory we had planned a trip across Africa into Liberia — it was another step towards realization of those youthful dreams I spoke of when we started our camp-fire tales—and were waiting for our rather extensive supplies to come up. For months we lazed, shooting only to keep the larder supplied. Then one day — it was August 14, 1914 — one of the post runners came into camp. I can see now the setting sun glinting on his polished shoulders, and the expression, half fright, half sheer excitement, in his coal-black eyes — when the pupils didn't disappear as he rolled them, leaving only the whites visible.

"What's the matter?" I asked, thinking some disaster had befallen his comrades.

"The English and the Germans are fighting," he blurted out, gesticulating.

The incredible news was not to be assimilated at once, but as I cross-examined him the truth developed.

"Where?" I asked, thinking at first it was some local clash.

"In Lindi and along the coast." His words came rushingly. "There isn't a boy left on any of the coast plantations."

The Germans employed thousands and thousands on these plantations, so that if this statement were correct something mighty big was on foot.

"We have seen none passing this way to their homes," I objected.

"They will be passing to-morrow, Bwana," he replied, with the assurance of certain knowledge. "I hurry, I run ahead."

I looked across at Hemming.

"It's come," he said, for of course we had heard of *Der Tag* and knew the Teuton dream of conquest; perhaps, indeed, his arrogant attitude of overlordship was more apparent on the fringes of the German Empire than it was at home. Certainly with a lot of natives under his control he had more chance to exercise his "superiority."

"It's almost too good to be true," I remember saying. For now and then we had talked of the possibility of Britain fighting Germany, and the fray seemed to belong to an age when we should both be too old to chip in.

We were both instinctively on our feet, stirred as though a bugle had called. In a way it had. I voiced the reason.

"We are in German territory, remember. We've got to get out. I shall join the first British forces I can reach."

"So shall I," said Hemming.

Men who spend years in the bush are not given to talk much, but that night was an exception. We discussed every possibility, in the end deciding to make for Lindi because we believed the British Navy were in control there. It would be a long trek, and dangerous because it was all enemy country, dotted with armed posts.

When we set out — just Hemming, Mare, and myself — it was as well we did not know what was to happen on the journey — that I should be gravely wounded, the others taken prisoner, and that weeks of fighting and dodging would elapse before I started on my second career, that of chief guide and scout to the British forces in Africa. In a way it was the same job, tracking through veld and mountain and jungle, with the exception that my quarries were no longer elephant or lion, but men who had become greater enemies to peace and freedom.

On breaking camp our first objective had been the British mission station at Masasi, but we never reached it. A native told us all the missionaries and sisters had been arrested the night before and taken to Lindi. To Lindi! That disposed of the stories we had heard of the Navy being in control there, and we decided that to proceed would be useless. No good fighting to gain the wrong goal. We turned back, deciding that our best plan would be to march to British Central Africa, or Nyasaland, though that entailed a journey of some fifteen hundred miles.

On arrival at Rovuma we received news that a column composed of two hundred Germans and askaris had left Newala early that morning, and were marching in our direction. We had no sort of doubt they were after us, for our camp was as well known to both natives and Germans as Charing Cross is to a Londoner, and we therefore took up a strong position on a small island in the river. Our camp was so situated that anyone approaching us in daylight could be covered at a range of a thousand yards, while we were invisible in thick bush.

We posted sentries, and all was quiet until about half-past ten, and then one of the guards reported to me that a big camp-fire was to be seen. I went to the edge of the island and knew that the Germans had arrived, for across the water fires were scattered over a large area, suggesting a camp of considerable size. It was Hemming's turn to go on sentry duty, but I lay awake with rifle, bandolier, and hunting clothes hung at my bedside.

At 2 A.M. Mare took his turn on picket, and Hemming and I lay and discussed the prospects of the morning. Our porters were sleeping in a sluit, where they had small fires to keep the mosquitoes away. Mare went on his first round of inspection, and when he was coming back I could hear him fully two hundred yards away, making a frightful noise with his number eleven boots.

"You are making a noise that can be heard a mile off," I called testily.

He pulled up and sat in a chair alongside the table on which was a hunting-lamp, and we were conversing when we got the biggest shock of our lives. It came by way of a yell from the boys in the sluit:

"The Germans are in the camp!"

We leapt to it. I tore out of my pyjamas, got into hunting clothes, and grabbed my rifle and bandolier, but did not have time to don my socks, boots, or belt. For by then the natives were stumbling over the boxes that were lying about the camp, and there was a regular stampede. I rushed to the scene of confusion with Hemming close by. Germans were swarming up the bank of the island right in front of us. They opened fire at once, and our first shots in the war were into their ranks — at some five paces. Our show of belligerency didn't stop them. They came rushing in, and we were gradually forced back until we were once more beside our table. Hemming smashed the lamp in order to extinguish the glare, but unfortunately the wretched thing caught ablaze and revealed us more clearly.

In such a light it was difficult to distinguish men from shadows and shadows from trees. Shots were continuous, and we kept darting from cover to cover. Suddenly I found myself alone. Hemming and Mare and all the boys had vanished somewhere among the darting shades. It was obviously an occasion of every man for himself — no chance of organized resistance. But in our talks through the night we had decided that if we were discovered, attacked, and driven out of camp we should make a stand amid a big clump of rocks, some four hundred yards away, near to the water. I dashed now for this vantage-point. It was a nightmare race. Twice I was bowled over — once because I barged into a tree, and again by stumbling over a branch that was right across my route. On that second occasion I was nearly caught, for, going down full length, I dropped my rifle, and as I groped for it scores of alien feet made ever-approaching sounds that interspersed the cracks of the owners' rifles.

I never got to that bundle of rocks. The askaris were there before me; they were everywhere. It was tragically clear that I was surrounded. Flashes lit enemy rifles in the darkness from every direction — except one. The river. . . .

I knew in that instant that I had to go into the water if there was to be any hope of escaping, and just then, as if to dissipate that hope, I was shot in both legs. At that moment a German voice cried raucously to the askaris, "Get him at all costs."

I knew the man who shouted that order, a Leutnant Wack, and saw him loom up a few yards away. The native soldiers made a rush. I plunged into the river.

My luck was in. A swift current was running, and almost immediately I was swept behind a dense reed-bank, which took me from the view of my attackers. But the flood of relief soon ebbed. In a few moments I had forgotten past dangers; I was oblivious of my wounded legs; all my attention was occupied in a new struggle to exist. With rifle in hand and a heavy bandolier round my neck, I was nearly drowned. Twice I went to the bottom of the river, but at last, kicking and spluttering, I managed to get my bandolier over my head and was able to keep my head above water.

It was when I began to feel for the bottom with my bare feet — and touched a boulder lying in the bed — that I first realized my hurts. A violent pain shot through me. Later I found the bone of my right leg was shattered.

Moving nearer to the bank, I sat down with the water up

to my neck. And there I stayed for fully an hour, both hiding and recovering, all the time in pain. Indeed, I don't know when I experienced such an hour of concentrated agony, for, though crocodiles did not worry me, an unruly school of little fishes did. They nibbled at my wounds, and as often as I pushed them away they returned, like flies about bad meat.

Just as daylight broke I crawled into the reeds to escape observation. Throughout the darkness the Germans had kept up their shooting spasmodically. I was actually about thirty yards below them; thus I dared not move, and the only interest that broke the monotony of that long, thirsty day was that I could often hear what the enemy were saying. I was glad to learn that they thought I had either been drowned or had died of wounds, from which I assumed they would look for me no more.

Sure enough, early in the morning they broke camp and went off towards Newala. Tension relaxed, but the lifting of the danger of discovery only made more real the plight in which I was. How could I reach help? I couldn't march; I had no supplies. I was alone. If any of my own party had escaped they would think that I was either dead or had got away; certainly they would not come scouring the river-reeds for me. It is true that Portuguese territory was only the other side of the water, and after hours of weary contemplation of my helpless isolation I was on the point of making a desperate bid to swim the Rovuma, when the pleasant rhythm of paddles at work broke the silence of the night. Still more good to hear were the voices of the canoe's occupants; they spoke the dialect of the local natives.

I called to them — and so started what must have been one of the longest treks ever a man made to join His Majesty's forces. Weeks were occupied over that journey. I was arrested and escaped. Desperation drove me to do things I would never have had the courage to do without that life-or-death urge that carries one through extremes. I spent weeks in the bush being carried by unwilling natives whom I had to tie together to prevent from leaving me. I spent more weeks in hospital. As early as the third day after the natives had paddled me over the Rovuma, with the pain in my right leg excruciating, I felt I could bear up no more. I was dead tired, and sick with agony. I lay down in a sluit where the sand was soft and comfortable, and at sunrise found I was close to a village. My leg was as stiff as a poker, and I could scarcely move; indeed, I thought I was done for, and gave up all hope of reaching safety. At the same time I knew only too well that if the Germans captured me they would put me up against the wall and shoot me without compunction, for I had fought against them as a civilian.

Vaguely I was aiming to reach Nyasaland, but it looked a pretty forlorn proposition to a fellow with a thousand miles' journey in front of him, limping on a shattered leg with the aid of a bamboo stick, and I was almost relieved when I was overhauled by a couple of Portuguese askaris who said they had orders to hand me over to the Germans. I let myself be arrested; it meant some medical attention maybe, and I argued that, since they would be certain to send me down to Palma on the coast, I should find a chance to escape during the seven days' journey. But the post Commandant at Ngomano, whither I was carried, had no medical supplies and, arranging porters and a stretcher, sent me off under guard.

For two days we proceeded, plans of escape ever accompanying my restless hours. Whether I should ever have succeeded in getting free and, had I done so, just how I could have used freedom I don't know; but fate stepped in before the journey was half accomplished. Incongruously enough, the kindly goddess came in the guise of a black face gone grey with fright. This belonged to none other than my gun-bearer, Saidi.

We were staying at a village, and I was laid on a mat out of the scorching sunshine under the shade of a hut. The askaris were eating under a big tree, perhaps thirty yards away, when I saw Saidi walk into the village. He came straight to me, began a tale of woe by telling me that he had seen Hemming and Mare. They had survived the fight, but had been captured and sent down the coast to be shot. He had been with them until three days previously. Then he heard that I was alive, and had run away in an attempt to find me.

"Have you any weapons?" I asked him.

"I have the old Lee-Metford, Bwana," he told me, "and twenty cartridges."

It was like a verdict of "not guilty" to a condemned man.

"Where?" I queried.

"Hidden in the kaffir corn, five hundred yards over there."

"Don't point," I snapped, fearful that my guards might suspect. Then, "if you can get that rifle and the ammunition to me unseen you and I will get clear," I added. "Go."

In fifteen minutes he returned and handed the loaded rifle to me without the askaris noticing his action. I promptly covered them.

"Put up your hands," I ordered. They obeyed. I then told them that they had to clear out and leave only the men who were carrying me. They agreed, claiming they did not wish to fight against me, for they knew me too well.

We travelled all the day until it was too dark to find a way through the bush, then camped. Next morning all the porters save two had deserted. It was a regular practice of the natives to clear out quietly when they were fed up; one often came across a Portuguese officer stranded far from help, his boys having deserted. It left me in a quandary, and there was nothing for it but to return to the village we had passed the previous day and collect a new supply of labor there. But the natives were wily; on arrival I found not a man in the place —

only women. The males, suspecting I might come for porters, had disappeared.

"They have all gone sixteen miles away to a beer-drink," the oldest female inhabitant informed me, but I felt pretty sure those menfolk were peering at me from the near-by bush. So I used a little stratagem. Since there were no men to act for me, I commandeered the ladies — twenty hefty specimens, who were compelled to carry my machila and some supplies I "requisitioned" in the village.

I smiled when, after half an hour, Saidi informed me that we were being followed by a man.

"Let him come along," I replied. In a few minutes the native was walking beside my stretcher demanding the return of his wife, who was helping to carry me.

"Take her place and she can go," I told him. He did so, the woman returning to the village.

Within the hour, in like manner, all my lady bearers had been relieved by their dutiful husbands!

At midday we were at the Lujenda river, and here I bathed my wounds and rested long enough to have the men plait ropes from the bark of trees. With this I bound them together, and added, by way of additional inducement for them to re-main on the job, that any attempt on their part to break away would be promptly answered by a rifle-bullet. It was a matter of life and death to me; why shouldn't it be the same for them?

For six nightmare days we proceeded in this fashion until my right leg became so stiff and painful that I began to think I should never reach British territory. The agony I was suffer-ing induced me to change my mind with regard to travelling straight through to Nyasaland, and I decided to alter my direction and proceed to Mazewa, on the Rovuma river, where there was a Portuguese fort in charge of one Da Costa, who was a personal friend of mine. He was a capable doctor and might be able to treat me. But a mile or so from Da Costa's boma Saidi, whom I had sent scouting ahead, returned with bad news. Da Costa had been raided by the Germans, and he and his wife had been shot as they opened the door. I went forward and found that the post had been burned out, that everything had been taken into German territory, and that Da Costa and his wife were buried inside the fort. This outrage upset my plans, and I therefore turned south, following the Chulesi river for three days, when I branched off, made for the top of the Emtapiri river, and from there crossed the dry stretch of waterless country to the Luwatezi. From that river I made straight for the villages of a well-known native chief, Mwembe.

They were not nice people hereabouts. Fort Valentine in this district was named after Lieutenant Valentine, who had been one of the officers sent to Mwembe's country. The savages captured him, took him to the nearest village, where they cut off both his hands, and then marched him through the villages in order to show the women and children what a white man looked like. He was then stabbed to death. But I had to go to these villages, for all my supplies had been used up and we had been without food for two days. We did not have to raid for food, as it happened, since we fortunately met a hunting-party and captured the chief, who, at the price of his liberty, filled our larder.

More days passed — anxious and painful. Gradually my worry in dodging askari patrols was overshadowed by the growing agony of my wounds. I found myself waking from unconsciousness and knew that I had fainted, and through periods of delirium, so Saidi told me, I issued queer orders, one of which was that they transfer me to a round bed without any corners! I suppose the movement of the machila (sometimes the bush was so dense the boys had to drag it on the ground) joggled my hurts.

Man-made Jungle

We came to the Livingstone Mountains, which trail up the north-east side of the Lake Nyasa — heavy climbing ahead — and now it was obvious something drastic had to be done about my right leg; either that, or I should succumb. It was in a terrible state. The two wounds had healed up on the outside, but the fractured bone was festering badly; while between the wounds was a big lump, and all up to the knee was black. The only thing was to open my leg and let out the pus and matter, otherwise blood-poisoning and death would result. I called Saidi, told him to get all the knives he could from the men, and, selecting the sharpest, I took it in both hands and placed it right on the lump between the two wounds. The mere weight of the knife was agony. Saidi held my foot, and I made the first cut. But the pain was so great that the moment I put the knife in I fell on my back and the knife slipped from my hand. The pain seemed to run all of a sudden right into my body, so that in agonized desperation I jumped up, got hold of my leg above the knee, and squeezed as hard as I could.

I almost lost heart when I looked at the wound, for I saw that, although I had made a big gash in my leg, only a very little blood, discolored and black, was running out. I must make another incision. It took me nearly five minutes to nerve myself to do so, and I then decided to operate in a different manner. I took a piece of cloth from the boys, folded it into a square of five inches, and wound it round the blade of the knife so that I could seize it in my left hand. About an inch of the point was protruding from the cloth. I placed the point on the open wound, and gave the handle a hard blow on top with my right hand. Again it knocked me over, but when I got up I saw a lot of pus was running out. I told Saidi and another boy to take hold of my leg in their hands and squeeze as hard as they could, so as to eject as much matter as possible. Next I immersed my leg in water and washed it thoroughly. For two hours the pain was excruciating, but afterwards I felt a great relief, and when travelling in the afternoon I fell asleep in the machila and felt much better when I awoke. Indeed, this was the first occasion on which I had slept soundly since I had been wounded.

At length we reached the border and entered British Central Africa, or Nyasaland. It was a vast relief to me to realize that I had regained safety. Not far away was the English mission station at Malindi, on the lake. While we sat down to drink water a priest from the station arrived on a cycle. He dismounted and walked towards me where I was leaning against a tree, and greeted me with, "Jambo, Bwana." I smiled, for I knew him quite well. The Padre then walked to the boys, and it was not until he heard from them who I was that he recognized me.

"By Jove, Pretorius, is it really you?" he ejaculated. "What is it? Fever?"

Half an hour later at the mission I saw myself in a mirror, and I could quite understand why the missionary had failed to recognize me. I looked a stranger even to myself.

It was twenty-six days since I had been wounded.

Down at Fort Johnston, on the lake, the doctor told me my crude bit of surgery in the bush had undoubtedly saved my life. Later he performed an operation on my leg, and for forty days it lay without feeling. Then it commenced to improve; I could tell when hot fomentations were applied. In three more weeks I was able to move to Blantyre for convalescence. Two more weeks and I could walk. In the end I made Pretoria, but before I reached the capital I had to sell all my ivory, and even pawn a gold watch and chain I owned, to cover expenses.

It had taken me nearly four months, after my first encounter with the enemy, to get where I could offer my services to the British authorities.

Then I was refused!

At the recruiting office they asked me where I had come

from, and when I told them they conceived the notion that I was telling tall yarns and must be a German spy! They didn't arrest me, but long after the war I discovered that a Miss de la Rey, sister of an Army captain, with both of whom I became friendly at the Fountains Hotel, where I stayed, was a Government agent set to watch me. She told me herself in the presence of other people that she had been instructed to report three times a day to the authorities as to my movements and what I had said. No wonder she and her brother made themselves so agreeable!

To say I was disheartened not to be able to enlist, after what I had gone through in order to offer my services, is not to over-state the matter, and it was a distinctly disgruntled son of the veld who turned his back on Pretoria and took train for that homestead at Nylstroom which he had not seen for nearly a quarter of a century. But if ever there was a dramatic turnover in my life it came to me there. A week or two had passed when, one day, a policeman accosted me in the street.

"You are Pretorius, aren't you?" he asked.

I admitted it.

"You must come with me to the Charge Office," was his curt order.

Wondering what further indignity awaited me — hardly caring — I accompanied him. And lo! everything changed. Here was a telegram asking me if I would accept service with the Imperial Government! And from that moment I lived in a whirl of surprises. Special coaches on trains, mysterious meetings with intelligence officers, even a special train pulled up by signal so that a telegram could be delivered to me as we approached Durban. I well remember the message. It read:

> With compliments from Admiral King-Hall on your arrival in Durban proceed immediately to C Shed Point.

And almost before I had finished questioning the guard of

the train about "C Shed Point" (he had never heard of it), another telegram arrived in similar manner.

On your arrival in Durban a special train will be awaiting you.

By such intriguing means I came to where, among other famous battleships, the *Goliath* rode at anchor. I was ushered aboard her, and she put to sea before a courteous officer had piloted me from my cabin to the ward-room, where dinner was waiting.

Such was the prologue to the drama of how we tracked the German raider *Königsberg*.

CHAPTER FIFTEEN

Chief Scout to Smuts

COMMENCING UNDER the ægis of the intelligence, as the African campaign against that resourceful German General von Lettow-Vorbeck progressed, I gradually became chief scout for our own brilliant commander, General Smuts, and, either on his instructions or with his approval, I spent weeks and sometimes even months at a time in or behind the enemy lines, gathering information. In view of the vaster panorama of the Second World War this is no time to give detailed descriptions of that other struggle against the aggressors, but the few incidents which make up this chapter are, after all, as much stories of the African wilds as of the African war. I was still following jungle trails, still the hunter, only the quarries were humans instead of animals.

Men left their spoor as did animals, and the practiced bushman could read the same story in the ashes of deserted camps as in the broken twigs and bent grass caused by the passing of a wild beast. One knew which way the enemy had gone, what was his strength, and how long since he had departed.

I well remember my first meeting with General Smuts. He took supreme command after the campaign had been in progress some time, and when he arrived, Major Shakespeare, of the Intelligence, took me over to see him.

His first questions (after some sly remarks about my poaching of elephants in German territory) were about Salaita. In front of half a dozen generals who were with him he asked my opinion as to how that hill could be carried. I was rather taken

aback and endeavored to laugh it off, saying that was a job for
generals, not for me.

But General Japie van Deventer spoke in Afrikaans to me,
explaining that they meant what had been asked, since I knew
the country well. Thus encouraged, I replied that the enemy
could be driven off the hill without firing a shot. "Salaita," I
pointed out, "is in a little desert where there is not a drop of
water to be found, and the Germans are getting their supply
from Taveta, a town eight miles away. I would parade six
hundred men in the afternoon so that the Germans could see
them. At the same time I would leave with a column in a
northerly direction until I got beyond the skyline, and then I
would turn back to the west, and by morning I would be at
Taveta. Once our troops are in Taveta, thirst would beat the
Germans."

General Smuts followed my reasoning, said it was quite a
feasible plan, and then remarked, "Taveta lies on the eastern
side of Kilimanjaro. Do you know whether the Germans have
any fortifications on Kilimanjaro? If so, they would attack
from our rear."

I said I would go and see. It was only twenty-odd miles
away. An hour later, with five men, I was on the way. We
crossed the Lumi river, thirty yards wide, to the south of the
German outposts at the lower end of the Zivane Swamps. Just
beyond the ford we reached the enemy road, where the grass
had been cleared, and crossed it, casting blankets over the
path in order to conceal our tracks. From here we started
climbing the Kilimanjaro foothills. The going was very hard,
for, in addition to the difficulties of climbing in pitch darkness,
we would frequently find ourselves in a deep hole, and at other
times bumped against great pieces of lava.

The men who were following me began to show signs of
distress and every twenty yards or so would get hold of my
coat and whisper that they had heard something in front,

suggesting we were blundering into the enemy lines. I took no notice of them, but pushed along as fast as I could, because, as I had explained to them, the hostile Wachaka tribe lived on the mountain slopes. These people had a very powerful chief, and the tribe, consisting of between sixty and seventy thousand, had already declared war on us. It was absolutely necessary for us to cover at least ten miles up the treeless and open slope of the mountain, get through the natives' fields in the dark, and by daybreak to be high up the mountain in concealing bush.

It was a freezingly cold night, and drizzling rain was falling, wetting us to the skin. When it became light a marvellous panorama was revealed. To the east of us, down the mountain, were the Zivane Swamps; to the north-west was an enemy outpost, a mission station a thousand yards away, filled with German soldiers. To the south-east I looked into the crater, Lake Chala, where I observed indications of another outpost, and up above towered the peak of eternal snows. About fifteen hundred yards away was a party of Germans on the edge of the thick bush. They were wandering about, and appeared to be working with helios and making signals. It looked as if they were on our tracks, which no doubt they had picked up where we had crossed the road. But they never found us, and, having carried out our inspection, we returned the next night, being able to report that there were no forts covering Taveta. The only menace to that town if we occupied it would be the outpost on Lake Chala.

On August 7, 1916, a move was made in accordance with the plan already outlined. General van Deventer left early in the afternoon with a mounted brigade, and moved rapidly away to the north-west, while at sundown an infantry brigade, of which I was the guide, departed from Mbuyini.

We all knew that one of our dangers lay in the hostile attitude of the populous Wachaka tribe through whose lands we had to pass. Dressed up in all their war-paint, their impis could be seen now and then. It seemed to me worth a risk to get on the right side of these fellows, and accordingly I offered to try to obtain a palaver with their principal chiefs. The plan appealed to General Brits, who commanded the infantry — lovable, good-humored Coen Brits, enormous of frame, of smile, of capacity for absorbing beer! "Go to it," he agreed, in his hearty voice, and he detailed a lieutenant and twenty-five men to accompany me.

After we had gone two miles we came to a number of native gardens where three of the Wachaka were working, and I proposed that we should capture these natives. But they fled, and, seeing us chasing them, an impi on the mountain-side became very excited, swinging their spears and chanting war-songs. I walked to within fifty yards of the warriors, when the two outside flanks moved to encircle me. I shouted at them to stop their war practice as I wanted to palaver with the principal chiefs, and they obeyed, two of the leaders coming forward.

"We are not fighting against black men, except the askaris," I said, "nor do we want any interference from you natives." It was essential that we should have a clear field behind us and no menace to our lines of communication, so I pressed my point home. "Put down your arms and you are safe. We are your friends, but if you disobey our soldiers who follow behind will exterminate you." Realizing I was deadly serious and that they might be attacked by a strong force, the chiefs agreed to return to their villages, and said that as soon as we had made the main camp at Moshi they would come in and lay down their arms. Almost at once the Wachaka dispersed in small parties in all directions, and this action, as General Smuts would confirm, assisted greatly in disposing of the danger of our being attacked by belligerent tribes.

Taveta was occupied without any real resistance, for von

Lettow-Vorbeck had marched from Taveta to two hills, named Reata and Latema, some way to the south. He had concentrated all his forces on this range of hills, which were not very high but were thickly covered with bush, affording a strong defensive position; to storm this range entailed crossing open plains without cover for a space of nearly a mile. During the afternoon the infantry attacked, and later in the evening the Second Rhodesians were sent in support. Heavy fighting at close quarters continued during the whole afternoon, and at several points our troops were temporarily repulsed. At one stage I saw our big guns being hauled back to safer positions, and for a while it looked as if the enemy were going to drive us back to Taveta.

At sundown orders came from General Smuts for me to get round the enemy flank during the night, reach the back of their lines, and ascertain whether the Germans were still sending up reserves and reinforcements. That was the sort of life I led for many months — often taking part in a battle, and then haring off in the night to gauge effects. On this occasion I found — seeing them with my own eyes — that the enemy was retreating. No reinforcements were coming up, and thus our Command knew von Lettow was only staging a rear-guard action.

I followed that retreat; General von Lettow-Vorbeck ably extricated his forces in the Kilimanjaro area, and they straddled the railway-line all the way down to Kahe, about seven miles distant. As they went a whole regiment of men pulled up the rails, taking away the fish-plates and bolts and sometimes dynamiting entire sections of the line. The bolts and fish-plates must have been thrown in the river, as we never discovered them; so that, in spite of our having captured it, the railway was of no use to us. For eight days I was away hidden in the bush, watching them ripping up the line, and ascertaining the enemy strength and disposition. When I got back to headquarters, at Moshi, the members of the staff were all surprised to see me, as they had received reports that I had been killed.

Almost immediately General Smuts sent me off on another job — to go along the Pangani river, and make a flying traverse of the country right to Buiko. I had to survey the country, for as soon as the rains were over there would be a big push, and, as we should be advancing through strange country where there were no roads, I was to map the best route, noting the most suitable points for temporary bridges, drifts, etc. On this trip I stumbled on a piece of valuable information. The country was occupied by the enemy, and one went warily. We almost flushed one German outpost situated on the banks of the Pangani river; once I had to betray my presence by shooting two troublesome rhinos within sound of an enemy camp; once I stood in what I thought was a deserted trench, when two German askaris rounded a bend and saluted me, thinking I was one of their officers! On another occasion I had to risk observation from an outpost because we just had to drink, and to do so meant crossing open ground to reach the river. We had an undisturbed fill, and then I made a fire, which had scarcely started when the askari shouted, "Look out; here come the Germans." I smothered the fire with my hand, and we jumped on the animals and tore off, continuing down the Pangani towards our destination, Buiko, seventy miles from Moshi. Three months later when I captured Schmidt and Linderkund, two German scouts, they told me that they were within an ace of capturing me at the river, and quoted some of the words that were written on the paper that I had used to light the fire.

The valuable bit of news came the next morning. We had slept on a big, isolated hill — a good spot from which to make observations. At sundown I had seen a big German camp, and so was astir with the first glints of day. To my amazement I saw the Germans come out and start musketry practice with rifles, firing away hundreds of rounds of ammunition at nothing but trees and boulders. This waste of cartridges astounded me, as we had been under the impression that the war would shortly end on account of the enemy's shortage of ammunition.

I remained on the hill until ten o'clock, watching this surprising spectacle, and when the Germans had retired to camp for breakfast I went down to their "Bisley" and picked up some of the cartridge cases. They were inscribed "Magdeburg, 1916." Where had all this ammunition come from? I could only surmise that a German or neutral steamer had managed to land on the east coast with supplies, and if that were so it was bad news for us, and meant the prolongation of the campaign. I squatted on the ground, deep in thought, and recalled that during my operations with the *Königsberg* my wireless operator had often stayed up at night picking up hundreds of messages that we could not understand because they were in German code. During the time that we were intercepting these radio communications I was told by naval officers that one of our cruisers, which had also picked up the messages, had found a German steamer in a small creek on the coast. The cruiser shelled the ship with incendiary shells, fired and sank it.

I did not learn the sequel until I captured Schmidt and Linderkund, and then they told me that the ship had run through the British blockade under a neutral flag with tons of supplies of all descriptions from Germany, including ammunition for big guns and rifles. With typical efficiency and foresight in such matters this ship had brought out divers, for it was obviously likely to be sunk. Our people, resting content in the knowledge that the ship was destroyed, went away. But the Germans, who had escaped to the mainland, returned next day with their divers and salvaged the whole cargo. For all the valuable ammunition had been packed in sealed cases.

Jungle Man

I always had my own little camp and personnel consisting of ten pagazis, or porters, who carried my goods, and my askaris, most of whom had been captured and had had their uniforms changed to those of the British askaris. I was therefore entirely independent of any column and slept at very few main encampments throughout the war, and then only for a night or two.

As I was on excellent terms with the native population I obtained reports from the various villages as soon as the enemy moved, and night and day natives arrived at my camp to give me information. The Germans knew this, and offered a big reward to anyone who would bring my body to them dead or alive. They also sent word to all the chiefs, saying that if they caught anyone assisting me he would be hanged on the nearest tree. By various other ways and means they tried to get the natives to work against me, but they were not successful.

But my immunity from wound, capture, or death was not due entirely to my knowledge of bush-craft, nor yet to any special genius to which my opponents could not lay claim. I had the help — many times exemplified — of an uncanny sense that I can describe only as psychic. I had a sixth sense which brought me such a definite premonition of danger that I have startled those whom I have been guiding by taking a sudden right-angled turn without being able to produce a logical reason. General Smuts knew of this strange awareness of trouble that came to me, and was conversant with several authenticated occasions when it saved my life and the lives of those in my charge. Here is one such occasion.

It was raining heavily on this particular evening as I rode back to the main camp to make a report. I had left my natives hidden in some kloofs well up in a high hill, a thousand yards above a German camp. My boys were instructed to watch for any movements along the various routes. I reached headquarters about sundown, and when I had reported the latest information concerning enemy movements the Staff insisted that I should stay there for the night, for it was pitch dark and I should have to go six miles back to my camp through the bush. I accepted the invitation with sincere thanks so far as dinner was concerned, but at nine o'clock saddled my horse and left, arriving at my shelter two hours later.

I had no tent at any of these camps. Tents were too easily spotted, and the shelters I constructed were of thin bush-wood and grass. I asked the natives whether they had seen any Germans about; they said they had not, and that there was nothing to report.

I was very wet and tired, and it was nearly midnight. I thought it would be safe enough for me to sleep through the night, so I undressed and put on my pyjamas, and as I was about to get into bed this instinctive feeling of approaching danger came over me, and I knew I must not stay there that night. I therefore dressed again, told the boys to collect my kit, and in a few minutes we were ready to move.

I hooked my arm in the horse's rein, and told one of the boys to go in front along a native footpath to the north, where about half a mile away we came to a deserted native village containing some fair-sized huts. On the far side was a range of little hills. The boys, who were wet and shivering, suggested that we should take shelter in one of the huts, but I told them we were not going to stay in the village but press on to the range of hills, and there we would sleep. Just as the boys spread my blankets we heard rifle-fire from the direction of our recently vacated camp.

I warned the boys to be on the look-out, as the Germans were almost certain to follow us. Sure enough, we soon heard the sound of a number of men advancing. They arrived at the village and banged on the door of a hut where some of the boys had sheltered. Under threats my wretched retainers emerged. I was watching from the corner of some kaffir corn, and observed that, having got their prisoners, the Germans sat down, took off their boots and puttees, and prepared to make themselves comfortable for the rest of the night. They got a surprise when I, and fifteen of my men who had kept with me, opened fire — so astounded that not one of them returned the fire! Instead, they rushed madly into the kaffir corn, leaving their boots, puttees, and haversacks behind, and the noise they made in the high, rustly growth sounded as if half a dozen elephants were stampeding through it.

It was in this same neighborhood, by the way, that one night I was surprised by a German patrol which endeavored to capture me. They got seven of my men, but I escaped and hid myself on a big hill a thousand yards or so above them. At eight o'clock the next morning I looked across a stream where the German party was camped, and saw them line up my seven men near a big tree. The enemy proceeded to hang them one after another. By such means the Germans registered their disapproval of natives rendering me any assistance.

On another occasion I was pushing through the bush, a mile ahead of my column, hoping to reach the Rufiji by next morning. On the map I had shown Colonel Morris, who was in command, the course which I wanted to follow. We hoped to surprise General von Lettow, cross the river with the whole column, without the enemy's knowledge, and then attack him on the other side of the Rufiji, which he occupied. Everything went well until we were within two miles of the crossing, when instinct warned me of impending danger, and I stopped.

Colonel Morris and the column asked me why I had halted, and all I could say was that it would be better not to follow the road we were pursuing, but to turn and march at right angles towards the west. All the officers on that march will bear me out when I say that I had this premonition of danger. We reached the river about two miles above the place origi-

nally chosen, and at sunrise the troops crossed by collapsible
boats and dug trenches. Scouting that day, I found that there
was a strong German position two miles below us, just where
we had originally intended crossing. But for that uncanny
premonition of mine we should have walked into hell itself.

Some good star has ever watched over me. I have heard
bullets buzz like swarming bees about my ears; I was betrayed
by natives on three separate occasions, and wriggled out of the
consequences; on one occasion I spent three months in enemy
country raising a native revolt against the German taskmasters, and was hunted, with a price on my head (which I
never dared lay to rest in the same camp two nights in succession); in numerous instances an unreasoning instinct of danger
had guarded me, and I had dodged certain death; and three
times deputies who took my place as guide were killed.

One of these substitutes was none other than that great
hunter Frederick Courteney Selous. I remember General
Smuts coming to me one day and personally countermanding
an order he had given me overnight. This was to act as guide
on an excursion to Behobeho; the new order was to lead the
Cape Corps to the Rufiji, while Selous was to take my place
on the other expedition. Lucky for me! Selous was shot by
a German sniper as he rode in front of his men. Mercifully he
was shot in the neck and died instantly — a very gallant gentle-
man, who had guided the Pioneer column into Rhodesia, and,
although well over sixty, was in the field again.

Captain Selous, of the 25th Royal Fusiliers, who had hunted
big game north of the Zambesi even before my time, was
buried close to where he fell in the African wilds, where the
lions serenade the spirit of a great shikaree. I think he would
have liked to die the way he did, in the face of the enemy, and
to be buried where he sleeps his long rest in the remote jungle-
land.

Another man who took my place was an Intelligence Officer

named van de Merwe, who was a pleasant, healthy-looking youngster, twenty-four years of age. I had received a telephone message from General Smuts instructing me to go to Makindu, to see whether von Lettow had reoccupied the place or not; but an hour later another communication ordered me to scout for General Beves when he moved forward to attack Merensky. Young van de Merwe was told off to scout in the Makindu district instead of me, and he was delighted to get the commission. I warned him the Germans would be on the look-out for us, and suggested he climb a kopje near the main road during the daytime and watch the traffic along the road. As soon as it grew dark he should, I advised, leave that kopje and climb into another, even though he felt sure he had not been seen by the enemy.

Ten of my askaris accompanied him, and after he left I started off with General Beves. Ten minutes after we had occupied Merensky's trenches one of the askaris I had sent with van de Merwe arrived. He reported that they had reached the position and had occupied it in accordance with orders. They had seen small parties of Germans passing, but van de Merwe did not feel inclined to move, for he was convinced that no one had seen him. Shortly before midnight, however, the askaris were awakened by the noise of a single shot fired among them. The boys jumped up and ran to van de Merwe, who was still lying in his blankets. They tried to wake him until they saw he had been shot through the neck, and was dead. The enemy had doubtless seen him when he took up his position, and later entered camp and shot him. We heard afterwards, from the local natives among whom the news had spread, that the Germans were elated, believing that it was I who had been liquidated.

It was a revealing fact that the natives invariably rejoiced over German discomfiture. The truth is, of course, that the Huns have only one method of rule — force. Sympathy, encouragement, and helpful instruction are, in their eyes, mere weaknesses, especially when dealing with natives. That is why they can never be colonists; that is why I was able to form a battalion (a thousand strong) of askaris from native prisoners we had captured from the Germans, and, by fair treatment, turn them into a loyal and valuable fighting force against their old masters; and that is why up in the Lindi area I found the natives sour and angered, suffering under German cruelty. In that rich soil I planted the seed of revolt — a revolt which helped materially to bring the district under our control.

I had been sent off to Lindi, some hundred miles up the coast, by steamer. This port, in the southern portion of the German colony, had been captured by us several months before, and it was reported that we had made no further advance because the Intelligence Department up there had been unable to obtain reliable information of the enemy's movements, chiefly for the reason that the natives were hostile. Many scouts had gone out and never returned. There was dramatic confirmation of the bad state of affairs the afternoon I reported to the C.O. there. While we were discussing the situation a man came running upstairs and burst in on us. He was thoroughly exhausted; sweat was streaming from his brow, and his face was black with marks of burned bushes which he had penetrated. He was obviously in a great state of distress and excitement, but clicked his heels together, saluted, and then said, "Sir, they have all got new boots."

We stared at him in astonishment, but he kept on repeating this cryptic sentence, and for a time we could get nothing else out of him. At length he explained.

"The Colonel and all his men have been killed," stammered Engelbrecht — for that was this scout's name — and he described how a hundred and twenty-odd men of the 25th Royal Fusiliers, who had been sent out to take a German outpost near a small lake fifteen miles north-west of Lindi, had been annihilated. Bad scouting. Engelbrecht had escaped by falling down among the wounded, and the Germans, thinking he was dead, walked over him.

I went to see the Intelligence Officer in charge at Lindi, Captain Dooner, who told me of the difficulties they were experiencing in obtaining reliable information. I asked him whether he had any native intelligence scouts in town, as I proposed to leave that night to reconnoitre the enemy position. Dooner's discouraging reply was that he had none; all of them had either been killed or captured by the enemy. Then I remembered my "foreign legion."

"What about the jail? Have you any German askaris in prison?" I asked.

"Yes," he said. "Quite a number of them."

We went over to the jail and paraded the prisoners. I selected sixteen askaris and talked to them, pointing out how much better it was to fight than stay in prison, and when I promised them the usual askari's rate of pay they were delighted, and promised to follow me faithfully. After long experience I could usually tell when tribesmen were speaking the truth or not. I was satisfied now. I also chose eight others as porters, and the next morning we started off towards the north.

That night we came to a jumbo, an under-chief's village, and here found that the road branched and that tracks of askaris were visible along both routes. The chief refused all information for a time, but in the end was persuaded to talk, and so I learned that along the road to the right, six miles away, was a German camp on top of the Makonde Plateau. He declared that climbing to the enemy position was a dangerous task, for the path was extremely narrow, and the entire range was flanked by precipices. I informed the chief that he was engaged to serve from that day, that I would give him five pounds per month, and that he was to keep constantly in touch with me and supply information. To this the local satrap agreed; friendly relations were established, and I started off along the road to the right.

During that night I reached the mountains and discovered a small outpost. Trekking farther to the west, we approached Makiwu, an important strategical point, where I found General von Lettow had nearly all his main forces concentrated, evidently ready to resist General van Deventer's advance from Kilwa. I also discovered that over the whole of the Lindi district were small, scattered German outposts, which sometimes had one white man and sometimes five, with the usual proportional complement of askaris. The main duty of these outposts was to compel the natives to cultivate all along the river-banks where anything could be grown, and there to plant mealies or beans for the feeding of the German columns. All the native population complained of the treatment meted out to them. They were arrested wholesale, and armed guards forced them, under pain of death, to till the ground.

I had a lengthy consultation with the Akida (Chief) of the district, asking him why he allowed small German parties to enslave the whole region in order to grow food for them in return for worthless rupee notes printed during the war. The Akida replied that his people hated the idea of being enslaved by the enemy, but, unarmed, they could offer no resistance. It was this talk that gave me the idea of organizing a revolt against the Hun. Was it possible to get the natives together in support of the scheme? Then was it possible to get the necessary arms and ammunition, and, further, was it a feasible thing to smuggle so much material past the enemy? And could it all be done without breath of it reaching von Lettow? It was a formidable undertaking, but it seemed to me to be worth the effort.

There and then I took the first step. I sufficiently engaged the Akida's interest to persuade him to summon a gathering of native representatives. That very night runners went through the jungle asking a chosen number of leaders to meet together on top of the western point of the Makonde Plateau.

That gathering would have satisfied in its atmosphere the most ambitious demands of a story-writer's imagination. It took place at midnight; and to it came the dusky chiefs, making their stealthy way from all quarters, by paths that sometimes plunged through jungle-land and, in the mountains, skirted precipices where a slip in the darkness would have meant a man's broken body lying hundreds of feet below. And all about the foot of the mountains were outposts of the Germans.

I addressed this native gathering, asking why, if they did not like being in the enemy's service, they stuck to their tasks. Their answers were all the same — they had to bow to *force majeure*. I learned there were two German Europeans and between ten and twenty-five askaris at each cultivation centre. If any refused to grow food they were shot.

"I will show you how to overthrow these tyrants," I assured them. "My people shall provide you with weapons, and the day shall come soon when you can drive your taskmasters from your country."

There were growls of approval.

"And," I added, "I will stay among you until the hour for attack arrives. It shall be at an arranged time of the moon, and all shall move as one."

The conference ended with the Akida and the chiefs being sworn into the British service, all being promised from that moment to receive full pay. After eight days' absence I reported to General O'Grady that as long as the natives were forced to cultivate for von Lettow the Germans would have supplies for an indefinite period, and in my estimation the most effective way of bringing the war to a conclusion was to strike at their local supplies, as they had no hope of smuggling anything in from the coast. I wrote to General van Deventer, describing what I had seen behind the enemy's lines, arguing that we could starve the Germans within a month if he was willing to provide me with as many rifles and as much ammunition as I wanted. He agreed to my scheme.

Back in the enemy country I summoned another meeting in the mountains, told the chiefs that plans were maturing, and that I should soon commence distributing arms and ammunition. I also pointed out that while I was among them they would have to feed me and did not minimize the danger they ran in doing this, for if the enemy found they were supplying me they would undoubtedly pay the extreme penalty. I suggested the following scheme. I would send a messenger the day before I arrived at a village, so that supplies could be got ready; and when I received them they would be paid for. The chief would then send a runner to the nearest German post, and inform the enemy that Pretorius had been there and had raided the village for food. The chief was to urge that the Germans should at once follow me, offering a good guide to follow my trail. In the meantime, while I was in the village I would tell the chief the position of my hiding-place in the hills, and the moment the Germans arrived in the village the chief was to send another swift runner to the appointed spot to let me know the exact strength of the enemy.

The chiefs and their people co-operated with me admirably, and by the pursuit of such tactics I remained for three months an uncaptured fugitive in this region. The natives who were working with me told the Germans that I had raided their villages, and that they wanted me captured, and the Teutons were completely deceived.

The smuggling then commenced. On some nights I and my men carried as many as two hundred rifles through the enemy area, and within a couple of weeks had enough rifles to arm two thousand men. Our plans were completed at a final meeting of the chiefs, when we decided that the signal for the insurrection should be the second day of the new moon, when all armed parties were to assault the German outposts.

The fundamental idea was to enter into the camps at midnight. Each attacking party was to consist of about a hundred natives, and when they were within thirty yards of the camp they were to fire their rifles and charge. I knew full well that the Germans, as they were in small parties, would fly for their lives at the first sound of a shot. The natives were then to set fire to the camps and scatter in the bush so that they would not be seen. The second night of the new moon I was on top of the Makonde Plateau, which was my headquarters. Every party was to report to me and to bring all the prisoners to my camp.

For the next three days I had one of the most exciting and thrilling times of my life. It was funny to see the local natives, each wearing an old sack with holes cut for his head and arms, armed with a rifle, full of martial ardor, some bringing in as many as three German Europeans, with the usual six or eight askaris. While the fighting was in progress the natives asked me if they could help themselves to the contents of the gardens, to which I agreed, and in consequence the whole of the district was soon as barren as a sand-dune.

During this period I had to move rapidly within a week from one camp to another, in much the same manner as a bird hops from one tree to the next, for the Germans sent out party after party to capture or kill me. On one occasion two companies converged on my camp, but — thanks to information brought me by my native spies — I wasn't there! Instead, I was squatted on a neighboring height watching a sharp engagement lasting an hour between the two companies of Germans, who each thought the other was my party.

When I returned to headquarters after the rebellion Captain Botha arrived with a letter from General O'Grady to inform me that I had been awarded a bar to the D.S.O. which had some time previously been conferred on me.

In a covering letter of congratulations General O'Grady wrote, "You most certainly are a thorn in the side of von Lettow." I deeply appreciated the compliment.

The pictures flit by. One, of an occasion when two bullets found my horse, and the poor animal fell dead under me. One, of a bad space when I had no food for three days and four nights. Several battle scenes, especially that assault on von Lettow's camp when he suffered eight hundred casualties, and we might have been annihilated but for a lucky way out I discovered while crawling between the fire of both friend and enemy. Yet another, of a scene in hospital, following a complete collapse which took place on one of my rare returns from enemy country to headquarters.

But there is one other I would particularize — a half-hour when I stood alone on a ridge and saw a plan, upon which I had built much, move, as it seemed, to inevitable disaster. I don't believe I took one normal breath during that half-hour.

The business began while I was in hospital. During that time my native spies, who were everywhere in the enemy country, some even in von Lettow's camp, continued to bring or send me their reports, and one day a man arrived bearing a letter that had been taken from a captured German messenger. It ran:

> Yesterday I had to fight with the enemy. I vanquished them and managed to capture their food, but their supplies, together with mine, can last only three days. I am trekking to the top of the Bangala river, from where I will follow it down to the cross-roads at the river.

The letter was signed by a Major Tafel, and was addressed to von Lettow himself.

Now, the cross-roads at the Bangala were only about two miles from the Rovuma river, and seventy-five miles from our position. I know the whole of this country, for it was here that I had poached elephants before the war, and I came to the conclusion that I should be able to reach the cross-roads before Tafel, that I could clear the natives out of the district, burn their supplies, and thus starve out the whole of Tafel's forces.

I wrote a note to General van Deventer setting out this plan, and sending him the intercepted message. Two hours later an orderly walked in and gave me a dispatch from the General which tersely read, "Herewith my car. Come immediately to headquarters." The hospital doctor cheerfully assured me that if I went out I should be dead in a week — but medicos, like other men, are fallible. The General tactfully ignored my illness and stated that everything would be arranged in accordance with my plans, and that when I reached the cross-roads I was to tell the native population on the Bangala that they could clear back to our lines, where those in need would be fed and assisted in every reasonable way.

The Bangala river was dry and sandy, and in most places we had to dig for water. Just near the cross-roads, however, was a big pond that collected water during the rains, and in some years the water was wont to last throughout the dry season. When we reached it this pond was pellucid and clear, so I knew the enemy had not arrived. I told my cohort to light a fire and prepare coffee, and while they were doing this I wrote two letters in Kiswahili instructing the natives to evacuate the district at once, as the enemy would be arriving that very afternoon. All the supplies they could not take with them were to be burned, and I explained that at five o'clock that afternoon I would come along the river-bank and any person found there would be placed under arrest. I really wished to frighten them, and therefore my instructions were couched in severe language. I knew them, and they knew me.

Even while I wrote sentries dashed up to say that the Germans were arriving at the pond. We cleared across the river, and half an hour later saw smoke rising from different directions. My scorched-earth policy was being executed — there would be no local supplies for Tafel. And, with the country clear of natives, Tafel would be unable to obtain runners or information through native sources of the movements of his own people.

I captured two German askaris that day, for Tafel was patiently waiting at the cross-roads for rations from von Lettow. My prisoners told me that they were looking for food, as they had been living on half-rations for many days. Tafel waited two more days, but those rations never came (he did not know the note he had written never reached von Lettow), and at length he moved on, following the Bangala river downstream for ten miles.

My little cavalcade pushed on, and gradually we got ahead of the enemy column. Several times, screened by kaffir corn, I caught a glimpse of them, so that I could see for myself, through binoculars, how weary and dispirited they were. Riding farther ahead, we arrived at a gorge, through which the river flowed noisily between high cliffs almost as straight as walls.

It was here I heard a shot — a shot which came *not* from the direction in which I knew Tafel's men to be, though for the moment they were out of sight. Then who was shooting? I had my doubts, and they brought me a sudden pang of anxiety that stabbed like a knife-thrust. My spies had told me that von Lettow was somewhere in the neighborhood. If Tafel and the Commander met, that would be farewell to my schemes to starve and capture the column I had been tracking — for von Lettow had supplies. With visions not only of losing my quarry, but also of being trapped between the two parties of the enemy, I bade my boys lie low in the undergrowth and made a mighty hasty scramble up those cliffs, hands and knees coming into hurtful play in the process. At the top a ridge ran still upward, and I ascended until once again I could see Tafel's men winding along a path beneath me. Then I looked to the other side.

There was another small army — von Lettow on his way to the Rovuma, never suspecting (thanks to a complete lack of native gossip) that his hard-pressed colleague was within a mile of him, wondering why succor had not come. But it looked as though they were going to meet. Not far ahead their roads would join; at the end of the very gorge upon which I gazed, standing almost breathless as though to breathe might somehow warn my enemies, Tafel would almost certainly run into the aid he so badly needed.

Sick at heart, I watched. Suddenly Tafel pulled up, a number of officers grouped around him. Some sort of consultation was proceeding. They stood right at the entrance to the gorge arguing, disputing, as I could see. Abruptly the disputation ended. A decision had been taken — and the column, all unknowing, turned its backs on salvation and marched on to its doom. It took a right-handed turn. The sense of relief was almost overwhelming — and then I chuckled in that excited manner one does when nerves are strained to the limit. It was indeed fortunate that Tafel had not heard that single shot — which I assumed to be a bullet sent after some sort of game for the pot. Had they heard it, or, perchance, had von Lettow's men fired again, Tafel's men would not have trudged despairingly on to the Makonde Plateau with empty stomachs.

I clambered down the cliffs, and followed along his trail with my natives. Only a mile had been covered when I came to a donga, where I found two men dying of hunger, while a native woman, one of the men's wives, was sitting with him, her eyes full of the stubborn resistance of the African to torture. The dying natives told me that for days they had not tasted food, and all Tafel's boys were practically at the end of their tether.

At five o'clock that evening the Germans arrived at a wide, sandy river. Their scouts had seen me and expected to be attacked; so they started entrenching themselves on the banks of the river. Great heaps of thorn-bushes were stacked in front of the trenches to obscure their actual position and to hamper an attack. That night I slept on the western bank of the water-course, about six hundred yards away from the enemy, in the dense bush, and the next morning I saw Tafel set off once more.

The column crossed the Rovuma that morning, and as soon as they did so they came in touch with the first natives they had seen for four days, who told them they had missed General von Lettow by a bare mile! The German Commander-in-Chief, von Lettow, had by now occupied Ngomano and had captured huge quantities of supplies and ammunition from the Portuguese garrison, who had run for their lives after their commandant had been killed in action. Tafel, who had been without food for three days, now ascertained von Lettow's position. He knew he would never reach him, so he dispatched a message to von Lettow, which I intercepted. It read as follows: "Am ceasing hostilities at 6 P.M. Wish to surrender on best possible terms." This message I passed on to General Hannyngton, in command of a brigade of the King's African Rifles, who was in the vicinity.

That afternoon of November 28, 1917, Tafel surrendered with all his men — 3400 askaris, nineteen officers, a hundred European noncoms, and a thousand porters.

That was the end of it — the whole of German East Africa had been occupied.

It was nearly the end of me too. My spirit was buoyant enough, for no greater success could have crowned my efforts, and General van Deventer was good enough to wire me his congratulations. "Am sending my car; come back to head-quarters," his telegram added, but, heaven above, when that car arrived there were a thousand damaged men needing conveyance to where they could get medical attention. Every vehicle was at once commandeered for that same purpose, and in the end I made a last effort to ride the thirty miles to camp. I was utterly whacked — never felt so near the finish in my life; and from that moment the remaining pictures of the African campaign are a blurred mixture of doctors, hospital stretchers, and nurses. I had gastric trouble and neuritis, and an artery in my lung burst. Once I had seven specialists gravely surrounding my bed. But I pulled through in the end after a few months. And there was one cheery spot I recall. In Dar-es-Salaam I had dinner one night with Tafel's staff. There a Captain von Brandis declared before all the other officers that he, and he alone, had wanted to continue down the river through the gorge that fatal day Tafel turned away from salvation, but he had been outvoted. And they all fully admitted that during the whole of that trek they had not seen a single native.

Conclusive enough testimony to the loyalty of my black friends, who had come to respect me — and I them — through many years of hunting and scouting.

CHAPTER SIXTEEN

Rogue Elephants of the Addo Bush

I HAD been scouting and fighting, struggling through bush, climbing mountains, and swimming rivers almost continuously for three years, and even to a person of my restless spirit it was calm and comfort to tarry awhile in Nylstroom. Here, in this pleasant little Transvaal town, where great willow-trees cast gratifying shade across the lazy streets, and with the noise of rippling water in my ears, I settled down for a short time and occupied myself by improving some property I owned there. But the nagging desire to scale the mountains, and see what lay beyond, still troubled my blood, and soon I felt that I must trek on to some other outspan. Before I had determined on my route I was visited by a Major Sillick.

"Still interested in hunting?" he asked me.

"Guess I'll always be," I smiled. "Was just contemplating going on safari."

"Good; come south," he invited, and went on to say he had a proposition to put before me. "And," he added, "I've travelled all the way from Uitenhage, down on the edge of the Karroo, to do just that."

We yarned. It seemed that down in the Addo bush, though it was near Port Elizabeth and other civilized parts, there was a bunch of rogue elephants that had taken a certain toll of life and more of property. I was surprised when he stated there were between two hundred and three hundred elephants there. "Yes," said he, "and they've been there since time began, and no one can hunt them out."

"Why not?" I asked.

"It's such a death-trap," he replied. "F. C. Selous, Sir Harry Johnson, the great naturalist, and Captain Maguire, who, as you know, was a mighty hunter — all these, individually, have visited the Addo and given the opinion that it is impossible to exterminate the beasts. I'd like you to look-see and give us your view."

Sillick was a member of the Uitenhage Town Council, and within their jurisdiction was a good deal of valuable land round about the Addo.

"It should be possible to shoot them," I ventured.

"Will you come and look the place over if the Administrator of the Province backs the suggestion?"

I said I would, and a week later I received a telegram from the Administrator, Sir Frederick De Waal, inviting me to Cape Town, "re Addo bush," all expenses paid.

On the way down I visited the Addo, and soon realized that if ever there was a hunter's hell here it was — a hundred square miles or so of all you would think bad in Central Africa, lifted up as by some Titan and planked down in the Cape Province. It was scrub, generally some eighteen feet high, and exceedingly thick. Once in this jungle it was seldom possible to see more than five paces ahead, and the jumble of undergrowth consisted of thorns and spikes of every description. A terrible country. Moreover, the class of elephants there — judging by their spoor — made them hardly worth shooting as far as ivory was concerned. Perhaps that, more than anything else, prompted me to tell Sir Frederick that I was not keen to undertake the job.

He understood that, but requested me (for a satisfactory fee) to outline a plan of campaign to get rid of the elephants. I did so, on the understanding that other hunters should carry out the work.

"But suppose," he insisted, "we cannot obtain such help, will you do it?" A little reluctantly I agreed; then I put the

"I could only see his head" (see p. 220)

"Dumbos" (see p. 220)

"Coerney" (see p. 220)

Practising Taxidermy in the Bush (see p. 237)

matter aside so effectively that I set about planning a safari on my own. I took ship up the East Coast for Durban, but hadn't proceeded farther when Sir Frederick wired me asking me to return to Cape Town as he had not been able to secure the services of anyone to tackle the problem of the Addo bush.

It so happened that about this time I was awarded the C.M.G., and I went to Pretoria for the investiture. Then I journeyed south and, finally, undertook to shoot the Addo bush elephants — a satisfactory contract being arranged.

Having purchased supplies, which included a .475 Jeffries double-barrelled rifle — a treasure of a gun — horses, wagons, and what-not, I established a camp in the famous Addo bush. No good, I thought, living on the outskirts, though all the local inhabitants assured me that to live inside would be fatal.

Well, it wasn't.

For three months I reconnoitred alone; I couldn't get boys to come with me. The place carried a sort of hoodoo, and no white or colored man would venture in. So with a rifle and a dog I scouted the bush in all directions in order to obtain a fleeting vision of the country, and to ascertain where the water-pools lay — a most essential strategical factor in an elephant war.

Throughout this period I was severely criticized by the public and the newspapers, all anxious to know when I was to commence my suicidal operations. Therefore it was with a grin of joy that one afternoon, after I had made a good survey of the country, I sent a telegram to Sir Frederick De Waal telling him I should start shooting the following day. To be perfectly frank, I will admit, as I told the people in my camp, that if it had not been for the reputation I had gained in the north I should have followed the example of Selous and left the Addo elephants severely alone, but as I had taken on the job I would rather have been killed than withdraw — such is the vanity of man.

I did manage to secure a few Cape colored boys, jail-birds of Uitenhage. These rascals were practically starving, for nobody would have anything to do with them, and so they were only too glad to accept any sort of work. The next morning, accompanied by a few of these schelms, I took my rifle and set off into the bush. After I had gone three miles the vegetation was so thick that we could not proceed farther in any direction, and then, quite suddenly, I saw an elephant standing within four paces of me, broadside on, and fast alseep. I fired, and that was number one of the hundred and twenty-odd elephants I killed during my sojourn of eleven months in the Addo bush. And, by the way, it was the only isolated animal I shot there; they moved about almost exclusively in big herds.

Apart from my own tracking, information came to camp now and then of the animals' movements, and in this way I was aware that a number of them were over Coerney Station way and set out after them.

Since hunting in these conditions was different from what I (or anyone else) had been accustomed to, I adopted changed methods, and improvised unusual means to meet unaccustomed circumstances. Who, for instance, would expect to find a ladder among a hunter's kit? . . . But I had one — a folding affair — and very useful it was, since I could not possibly climb the fragile trees of the bush, but one could mount to a rather wobbly observation-post by poking the ladder up among the swaying branches.

I soon picked up the elephant spoor, and saw that there were sixty or seventy of them, heading straight for Coerney Station. It was evident from the tracks that the elephants were close, so I put the ladder against a bush, climbed it, and although I could not actually see the beasts, I located them, by signs of movement, some hundred yards ahead.

We crept forward, but not for long undetected. The

elephants got our wind, and at once they came thudding our way, trumpeting noisily. I threw the ladder against a bush. All the boys vanished into thin air, except that I managed to secure the one who carried my cartridges. I forced him to remain with me, and told him he was to stand on the lower rungs, and hand me the cartridges as fast as he could when we were attacked. He had some guts, that boy, for he obeyed my orders while the elephants came on, squealing like a million scorched fiends. The first one I saw through the bush was not ten paces away, and I let drive.

I killed four of them in succession as they were right round my ladder and wounded a fifth. The rest of the herd dashed off towards the south, but that wounded beast struggled towards the railway, which was not far away. We could hear the natives working on the line and talking, and the animal ambled straight towards them.

I was afraid it might reach the railway people before they saw it coming, and that they would be killed, so I started forcing my way through the bush on its trail as fast as I could, still followed by the boy with the ammunition. Suddenly I came on the elephant. Its progress had been slow, but the bush was so dense that I had to turn out of the track before I was able to get alongside the beast. Even then I could not see it, as the undergrowth was the type we call the "num-num bush," which was practically impenetrable. This num-num bush is a hideous mess of long and diabolical thorns, its stem prolific and intertwined after the manner of a bramble. I was within three paces of the animal before I saw him. Having regard to its position in relation to myself, and from previous experiences, I knew that the only thing to do in the circumstances was to smash the spine (for the moment an elephant's spine is broken he collapses on his haunches), then run up its broad back and dispatch him with a bullet right in the neck, breaking the vertebræ. I would not, of course, advise a novice at the game to attempt this, as one must know how far to go up that spacious back, for an elephant's trunk is long and one may quite easily be grabbed and flung to the ground.

When I had got in my spine shot, and saw that the elephant had sat down, I ran up his back and killed him with a shot in the neck. As the great carcase collapsed in death it slipped forward, and, since I did not have too good a foothold, I fell forward right in front of his head. Fortunately for me, the elephant's dying rage was over.

Through the boys the story of this episode was spread abroad, and I remember being particularly amused when listening to a highly colored version of it one day as I sat in a train coming from Port Elizabeth, where I had been to buy some camp equipment. I had to change at Barkly Bridge, and was waiting for my connection to Addo, when a freight train came along, and I asked the station-master if I could travel by it. He said I could, adding that there were a few other passengers. I jumped into the guard's van, and inside found two old grey-beards, one an Englishman and the other a Dutchman. As we pulled out they started talking about me.

The old Boer asked the other if he had seen the man called Pretorius, who was supposed to be killing elephants in the bush. The other promptly went off into an excited account of how I had climbed up the back of a live elephant and then shot him behind the neck. They argued about this yarn — and argued; but I said nothing.

About a week later, however, I went to the Addo Hotel, where I was introduced to Mr. Nett-Harvey, the proprietor, and there I met these old fellows again. They were sitting next to me, and the moment Nett-Harvey told them who I was they jumped up and exclaimed, "You blighter. You sat in the van with us the whole afternoon, and did not tell us who you were."

For a time I had a weekly bag of three, four or five elephants, but at the end of the month I struck a blank patch. It was borne home to me that to follow the Addo elephants and shoot them one at a time was going to be a long and tedious job. And so I resolved to change my tactics: pursue them, and shoot as many as I could in charges before they broke away.

The first day I went out after this it happened that there ˋ ere eyewitnesses to the success of operations. That morning at sunrise two men entered camp and introduced themselves as Norton and Bloomfield. Norton was a man who was well over six and a half feet in height, and was a wealthy farmer who lived just outside Oudtshoorn; while Bloomfield was a brother of Major Bloomfield, V.C., who once had come with me into the trenches on the Rufiji, and was also a farmer. They told me with disarming candor that they had heard so much of my quick-firing they had decided to come and see for themselves.

"We have invited ourselves," they said, "and, if you will allow us, would like to follow you into the bush, and if one of us runs away you can shoot both of us."

"You are very welcome; I have an open camp for anyone to visit," I replied.

I found that the elephants had trekked south, and after we had marched through the bush for three miles we came on fresh spoor, and about midday I halted the party.

"Can you hear them?" I asked my guests. They listened. A rolling bourdon like the sound of waves in caverns, accompanied by a noise resembling drum-beats, came from a distance through the jungle.

"I can't place it," said Norton, and they would hardly believe me when I assured them the disturbances were occasioned by the water rumbling in elephants' stomachs and the flapping of their huge ears.

"Some indigestion," grunted Norton. "How far away are the pets?"

"Thirty to forty yards," I told him, whereat they suddenly tensed.

My double-barrelled rifle had an ejector, by means of which, after I had fired either one or two shots, I had just to touch a lever and the empty cases were automatically ejected. I told one boy, who I thought was devoid of fear, to load for me, as I never loaded myself when I had to do quick-firing. He was also to bear my cartridge-case. I always carried five cartridges slipped into loops on my shirt in case of emergencies or in case a boy ran away when elephants were charging.

I instructed the party that none of them was to follow me, and, whatever they did, they were not to run away in different directions in the event of a charge, as they might dash into other elephants they had not seen.

Bloomfield took out his watch, and said: "I am going to time you from the first shot."

I walked towards the animals, accompanied by my boy. Parting the bushes carefully in order not to make a noise, I was able to come within a few paces of the herd, and I saw in front of me a big elephant standing broadside on, fast asleep. I fired. The big elephant dropped stone-dead, and all the others stampeded towards me. The position was such that very quick firing was necessary. I dropped five elephants in quick succession, each with one shot. But now the other elephants were streaming by on both sides, trumpeting as loudly as they could, and I realized that the other members of the party were in danger.

When I had shot the fifth elephant the animals surged round me like a solid wall. I held my rifle out waiting for more cartridges — but none came, and when I looked round I saw that the boy had vanished with my ammunition. Luckily I had a last round in my shirt, and just as I was in the act of loading one of the elephants made a most determined charge. I thought for a moment he would be over me before I had the cartridge in the breech. I put up my hand; the elephant saw me and hesitated a moment. This second gave me a chance to load, and I dropped him. Then I called out loudly to Norton and Bloomfield: "Look out. My cartridges are finished."

The others were firing as fast as they could as the elephants passed, and I heard Bloomfield shout at the top of his voice: "Thirty seconds."

I did not look to see how many elephants had been killed, but ran towards the party to assist them if they needed help; but when I arrived there the last elephant had already passed, and I found they had actually killed one. Needless to say, they were exceedingly proud of their bag. We went to examine the place where I had stood, and we found that six elephants had been killed with as many shots. Norton and Bloomfield declared that this must certainly constitute a world's record. All I can tell you is that it was a treacherous position to be in, and I would certainly not care to repeat the experience. They had been lucky. Arriving in the morning, by three o'clock they participated in an elephant hunt the like of which many men who had spent hundreds of pounds on safaris had never seen.

By now the elephants had become disturbed, and nervous of me. They fully realized that a human being was bent on their destruction, and I had hard work locating them. One day it was five o'clock in the afternoon before I reached the herd. I managed to get within very close range indeed; in the whole of the Addo bush I had never shot an elephant that was more than ten yards distant, and, in fact, most of my shooting was done when I was right on top of them. That afternoon I shot two elephants before they could get away. I was very fatigued, and so were my boys — who had been carrying water and food the whole day. Camp was far distant, so I told the boys we would wander around until we found a pan — a shallow depression in the open veld that fills with water during the

rainy season and is dry in the winter months. We walked away
from the dead elephants, looking for a clearing where we
could lie down. After I had gone two hundred yards — with the
boys in front of me clearing the bush with their hands while I
walked behind — I heard the snapping of branches behind me.
I looked round, but saw nothing and went on. A little farther
and we came to a pan devoid of all vegetation. We sat down,
and just as I put my rifle on the ground I heard the branches
crackling again, and on looking back saw a very large elephant
entering the clearing on the opposite side. He had his trunk
high in the air, and as soon as he saw us he trumpeted and
charged. I was just in time to grab my rifle, swing round, and
shoot him where the trunk joins the head. The elephant spun
round like a top — for he had been coming at full speed, and
the moment the bullet struck him he was thrown a good two
yards off his path — and then almost instantly dropped dead.

The next morning I told the natives to open the elephant's
head, for I wanted to see how far the bullet had penetrated. I
found that it had gone through the brain after entering the
head at the trunk, and had then entered the vertebræ. The
missile travelled along the vertebræ for about a foot and then
branched off, for we found the bullet in the elephant's liver.
The whole of the spine had been neatly cut in two for the
length of the bullet's travel. It is difficult to appreciate the
striking force of a .475 Jeffries rifle, but I consider that this
weapon is undoubtedly the most effective in the world for
elephants. The price of such a rifle just after the last war was a
hundred and fifty guineas, and I consider the weapon to be
worth every penny of the money, particularly to a man whose
very life depends upon the accuracy of his gun.

CHAPTER SEVENTEEN

Dumbos

BABY ELEPHANTS are lovable beasts, and in the Addo I captured several. It was a pleasant interlude to shooting. But one or two of them provided me with some excitement.

I knew that there would have to be some one to look after the Cape boys in the job of preserving specimens, and I had therefore applied to the Minister of Justice to grant leave to a policeman from Uitenhage, one van der Linde, whom I had known before I had set out on the elephant trail, so that he might assist me.

The first time he came out with me we travelled until three o'clock before getting sight of the beasts. They quickly got our wind, and I was able to drop only one of them. I knocked down another, but the animal jumped up again and cleared after the herd. Although every one was tired, I told van der Linde that we had to follow the trail, as I was bound to finish off a wounded animal. I walked ahead, and he followed immediately behind me with my second rifle, in case any mishap might occur to my Jeffries. Invariably an elephant makes for the densest part of the bush, and in consequence we had to follow the spoor by forcing our way through well-nigh impenetrable barriers, with our hands before us to shield our faces. After half a mile we heard a terrific squealing a few yards in front. I pushed forward, only to come face to face with a baby elephant. Instantly I lowered my rifle, for I did not want to shoot the little creature, but young Dumbo charged right at us and tried to bump me with his head. I side-stepped him, and he lumbered on. I grabbed his tail, and, as I hung on, he dashed through the Cape boys, scattering them in all directions.

I was handicapped by the fact that I had my rifle in my right hand and did not want to drop it, for there was a likelihood that the baby would lead me straight to the herd, in which case I should have to let the infant go and face an attack by the parents.

I yelled for help, but neither van der Linde nor the others came to my assistance, and after we had gone fifty yards the elephant suddenly swung round. I was so unprepared for this that I was lifted off my feet, hurled through the air, and fell on the flat of my back with nearly all the breath knocked out of me, while the baby ran at me with his head lowered, side-stepped, and dashed past me. I scrambled up and again caught his tail. But now I was sure the herd had departed, otherwise I should have been attacked, and so I dropped my rifle, and still calling "Come and help me!" held on to the youngster like grim death.

No one appeared, but, fortunately, after we had gone another two hundred yards through scrub and thorns we reached a pan. Here in the open I was able to get a proper grip of the elephant. To do so I caught hold of the top of his trunk with my right hand, and with my left I grabbed the trunk lower down. This did not arrest his progress, but made him go round in circles, screaming with fury all the time.

At this stage two of the Cape boys arrived. The elephant was still staggering forward, while I was streaming with perspiration and nearly exhausted. I shouted at the two boys to get hold of the unruly infant. They collared him round the neck, while I rested for a few minutes. They struggled with him, but could not hold the wretched creature, and he set off for a patch of num-num trees at a lively pace. I bellowed at the boys to hang on to him and to catch him by the tail. The moment they did so they were dragged right through the bush, while I rushed round to head off his retreat. When he emerged — the two boys still hanging on — I got my arms round his neck once more, and then van der Linde turned up. There were now six of them grabbing the elephant and trying to stop him, and all the while his screams were deafening.

We were in the open now, and not far away was a homestead owned by a Mr. Philip Fourie. When we came to the lands about a mile from the house I told them to let the elephant go. I ran ahead, and the elephant promptly trundled after me. He tried to bump me with his head in order to make me accelerate my pace, but by this time he was a very tired baby, almost as fatigued as I was, and when we reached Fourie's house, an hour after we had captured him, he was as tame as a kitten. In the yard I chatted with Fourie, while the young elephant stood peacefully beside me, just like a huge puppy. It is really remarkable how they take to the first person whom they see and smell; they always stick to that individual, for they are creatures of great sagacity and long memory.

As our camp was so far distant I asked Mr. Fourie if we could stay there, to which he replied that he would be delighted; and, moreover, he gave us a store-room in which we put the elephant. Mr. Fourie and his brother were curious to ascertain the elephant's strength, and we agreed to test it. Obtaining a strong manila rope, which was used for a windlass, we tied it round the youngster's neck. Fourie and his brother held on to one end while I walked away. The elephant followed me, and Fourie and his brother, though both big men, might as well have been a couple of ants for all the effect they had on the elephant. Although they dug their heels in, they soon toppled over as the elephant walked unconcernedly forward. And remember, "Coerney," as we christened our captive, was only four feet high.

Four days later I tracked a herd travelling at a fast pace towards the south. I kept close on their trail for nearly four hours. They went down a steep kloof, and as they climbed the other side I sighted them and killed three. Another was badly

wounded, so I ran after him to administer the *coup de grâce*.
I could only see his head, and, since it was impossible to get in
a side shot, crawled through the thicket in front of him. Just
as I reached the danger line he let rip with his trunk, missing
my head by a hair's breadth and sweeping my hat off — which
he grabbed, stuffed into his mouth, and chewed for a few
minutes before spitting it out. I finished him off, and regret-
fully seized the remnants of my headgear. While I stood there
contemplating the animal I heard screams, and, looking round,
saw a baby charging towards me. I put a hand on his forehead, and side-stepped. He again turned on me, and since the
bush was not too thick, I said to the boys, "Pick up the stuff
and follow me."

I walked in the direction of the camp, closely followed by
the elephant, who every now and then would bump me with
his head if I was not going fast enough to please his wishes.
This certainly is the easiest way to catch a baby elephant. If
the bush is not too thick, set off for camp the moment he comes
at you. For the first mile or so he may give trouble, but after
that he will follow as tamely as a dog.

Fortunately for hunters, a young elephant does not realize
the strength of its trunk. I caught seven baby elephants in the
Addo bush, and if one of them had employed its trunk to tap
me on the head I should not be alive to tell the tale. This
particular baby rubbed itself against me every time I stopped,
and followed me into the camp meek as a lamb. We named
him Addo, and he and Coerney had many a peaceful meal
together.

Speaking of meals, the greatest difficulty in rearing a baby
elephant is to discover and maintain its correct diet, as it is
extremely susceptible to diarrhœa, and dies very quickly.
Although the milk from an elephant looks thin and watery,
it is by no means weak. Once I had some elephant's milk
analyzed. The certified report proved that the milk contains

at least 100 per cent more albumin than that of an ordinary cow. To find a substitute for that is no easy matter. Experience has shown me that it needs a gallon of cow's milk, half a pint of cream, the whites of two dozen eggs, and four pounds of boiled rice to provide a young elephant with an average, naturally balanced ration.

During that same week of Addo's capture I found that the elephants had trekked to Sundays river, so we set off after them through waterless country, and reached a portion of the herd that afternoon. I got to within a few paces of one elephant and fired an ear shot, which, if accurately placed, causes the animal instantly to sink on its knees. When any other animal receives such a shot its head slumps forward to the ground, but an elephant's head remains erect, for it has a number of sinews about two inches wide between the skull and the neck, and these keep the head stiffly upright, three feet or so above the ground, after death. Even if you approach the animal a day later you will find that the head is still rigid, with all the appearance of life. So lay this particular animal when I came up to him. This was one of the rare occasions on which I shot just one elephant out of the whole herd; in practically all other instances I killed three, four, or even five before the remainder broke away.

This elephant was a female, and it was not until we came right up to the animal and stood beside her that I noticed a little one standing under its mother's head. It was trying to drink; but when it saw me it emerged under the maternal neck and smelt me. As I walked to the road leading to Mr. Jack Harvey's farm the baby docilely followed me. Rain was falling heavily, and we were wet and muddy. When we knocked at Mr. Harvey's door he at once invited us to enter. It was eight o'clock at night, and we did not feel inclined to go in, for we were in a bedraggled state, and I had only wanted to ask him if he knew of a short cut to our camp.

"If I enter, the elephant will follow," I said to Harvey. But he replied that it did not matter, and insisted that I should come in. The elephant followed me into Harvey's sitting-room, where he soon made himself an utter and complete nuisance. Believe me, an elephant, even if it is young, in a sitting-room is more disturbing than a bull in a china shop!

On the way home that night we detected the presence of a large number of elephants just ahead of us. In that almost sepulchral darkness I did not want to shoot, and ardently hoped the animals would leave the road, for we were cold and miserable and wanted to get to camp. We tried shouting; eventually I fired a few shots in the air, but not one of the herd moved. The more noise we made the more did the elephants trumpet in a challenging chorus. I am fully convinced that they knew they were my superiors in the dark, for they would not budge an inch, though in daylight they fled as soon as they scented me.

With great difficulty we managed to branch off, outflank the herd, and pick up the road again near the camp. Meanwhile the baby had stayed close to me and had not made the slightest attempt to join the herd.

I sold Addo to a circus proprietor, a Mr. Boswell, at a price of three hundred pounds. The day the deal was concluded Boswell said to me, "Is this elephant tame enough for us to exhibit to the people at to-night's performance?"

"Yes," I declared; "we'll bring him along."

Where they were pitched was some miles away, and I started about five o'clock driving in a spider drawn by two smart steeds. Addo had departed in the care of two Cape boys, while a Miss D'Arcy and Miss Allan, two visitors to my camp, accompanied by van der Linde, set off ahead of me on horses. On a steep dip of the road the dissel-boom jerked out, the horses pulled the reins out of my hands, and I catapulted out of the cart, landing on my knees. When I lifted my head I saw both horses still trotting along the road. I got up and ran after them. Unfortunately, just as I grabbed the reins the horses snorted and bolted down the narrow road. I at once thought of the girls in front and feared they might be hurt. I raced on for all I was worth.

After a quarter of a mile or so I heaved a great sigh of relief, for I found the two girls safe and sound standing on the side of the road. They told me that van der Linde had nearly been killed, as he had turned his mount broadside on to stop the two stampeding horses and in a flash had been knocked down, horse and all. He had speedily remounted and given chase. Running on, my next encounter was with the two Cape boys who had been in charge of the baby elephant. But Addo was not there; the bolting horses had stampeded him! The road to Addo that afternoon took on the appearance of an African chariot race, with an elephant in pursuit of two maddened horses.

Nearly at Addo Station I found van der Linde with the two horses. They had run into a barbed-wire fence and had become so entangled that he had managed to capture them. I asked him where Addo was, but he did not know.

It was dark now, and I walked to the road, struck a match, and saw that the elephant spoor was there all right. As I approached the station I saw a vague form that looked very much like the animal enter the yard. And there I found him, standing in a corner, peaceful and, I fancy, reflective. The moment I came up to him he lifted his trunk, smelt me, and followed as I walked out.

The Boswell galaxy of talent had already given a few turns, and now the circus proprietor requested me to enter with the elephant, for he had announced to the audience that they were about to see an elephant straight from the wilds. The placid unconcern of an elephant once he is truly tamed is remarkable. This little chap went among hundreds of people and took as little notice of them as he would of pebbles. He followed me right round the circus ring, and was as uninterested in the other animals as he was in the audience.

I then told the onlookers to stand in front of their seats, and I would demonstrate the wonderful powers of scent possessed by the animal. I assured every one they would be quite safe. The people rose and crowded together, while I tried to get away from the little beast. I mingled with the audience, turned this way and that, but Addo found me every time, and entirely ignored every other person in that not inconsiderable congregation.

CHAPTER EIGHTEEN

Tragedy in the Bush

ONE MORNING in 1920 General Ravenshaw, General Dawson, and Mr. Fitzroy, a son-in-law of Lord Buxton, Governor-General of the Union, arrived at my camp. Before four o'clock that day General Ravenshaw was dead.

The two Generals were British officers who had been captured by the Germans during the First World War, and had suffered terrible hardships in German U-boats, which had been their prisons for many trying months. Before they came to me I had received letters from Sir Frederick De Waal in which he said that the Government wished to know whether it would be possible for me to give these two men a holiday in my camp, as they were both keen sportsmen and would like to hunt elephant. They were, of course, very welcome.

On the morning of their arrival I told my boys to saddle three extra horses, and I set off for Sand Flats Siding (the nearest railway) to meet them. Two miles along the road I came to a spot where a leopard had killed a bush-buck and dragged it across the road. The spoor was quite fresh, and the story told by the tracks was clear to read; the leopard had taken the bush-buck to hide it in bush. I dismounted and followed the tracks a few yards. I had no weapons with me, however, and, as I saw nothing of further interest, returned to the horses and hurried off to the siding. My visitors were waiting, and, mounting, we rode back to camp for breakfast. On our way I pointed out to them where the leopard had dragged the bush-buck across the road, and they were quite thrilled to see a trace of African wild life so soon after leaving the railway station.

When breakfast was over I said to my guests, "If you'll excuse me I'm going to see if I can find that leopard." Immediately they asked to come along, and we all set out, accompanied by some of the boys and my two Alsatians. When we reached the place of the kill I unleashed the dogs, which bounded forward and disappeared. I followed them, and had gone no more than twenty yards from the road when I noticed a tree from which a large twig had been broken. I picked it up, showed it to my visitors, and told them that a herd of elephants had passed only five minutes before. This information intrigued them considerably, and we decided to follow the herd. Very soon the Alsatians began to yelp noisily. These dogs have a special bark when they locate an elephant; thus I knew they had come upon the herd and were driving the animals towards us. I told my guests to remain immediately behind me.

Here again I proved how acute is the scent of an elephant. The animals were coming directly our way, but within a few yards of us they caught my wind, wheeled round sharply, and raced off in the opposite direction. I could have got in a shot or two, but I was anxious that my three companions should have a chance, and as the elephants turned I shouted, "Fire!" Unharmed, the animals cleared off into the bush. Experience had taught me that the most effective plan to adopt in such circumstances was to approach close to the pursued elephants, for they clear the bush as they run and create a wake of parted bushes along which one can continue the pursuit before the bushes close again. It saves a lot of time and trouble.

I proceeded on this open-and-shut clearing a few yards behind the elephants, and never looked back. But after I had run for some five hundred yards I turned and, seeing no one behind me, stopped. Where were the others? Minutes passed while I stood there listening to the departing elephants as they tramped through the bush. Then two men came stalking in front of a ragged bunch of the boys — General Dawson and Mr. Fitzroy.

"Where's General Ravenshaw?" I asked.

"Coming along," was the comforting answer.

But the practiced bushman is always a little anxious if a stranger is wandering alone, even though he be near; there are so many ways of tumbling into trouble, especially, as now, if there are wild animals about.

"We'll hang on till he catches up," I said, devoutly hoping the soldier hadn't got lost. It's a simple thing to do just that — and there is nothing more devastating to the nerves than to be "bushed." That Addo jungle might not be very extensive, as mileage goes in Africa, but it was as thick as any I know, and in a few paces a man could be lost. In fact, this had happened only just prior to my arrival there. A honeymoon couple left the train at Coerney Station and went strolling into the bush. They were never seen again, and search-parties found no trace save bits of clothing.

I reprimanded the boys for leaving the General behind, for they knew he was a stranger.

"Spread out," I ordered them. "And shout."

They disappeared, and soon "Cooees" were to be heard. Surely those should reach the ears of the General. But there was no answer. The heat sat on our heads like a blanket; I remember even to-day the snaky trickle of perspiration that irritated the back of my neck. It was hot almost beyond bearing; and still, still as the grave.

We all started shouting; you know how excitement and fear will creep from one to another in a crowd, however small. The silence of the bush in answer was ominous. I know my throat was parched, not altogether with the shouting, and I suspected the others were the same. So I led the way to a windmill that was not very far away, and there we drank. Meanwhile I told

227

two boys to follow our trail back to the point where we had commenced to track the leopard, for I still had hopes that Ravenshaw would be sitting down somewhere in the bush, probably tired after running, and, conscious of the fact that he had lost his way, had decided to remain where he was.

At the well we had a good drink, and then lit cigarettes and had a smoke. Suddenly, as we were sitting there, my dogs dashed up, lapped up water, and then raced back to the bush again. We followed our trail to the starting-point and, shouting loudly, went backward and forward at least half a dozen times. Still no response. The two Cape boys also had disappeared, and I therefore came to the conclusion that they had taken Ravenshaw through the bush into open country where he could obtain some shooting, or else return to camp. General Dawson repeatedly expressed fears for the worst, but I consoled him with a quite justifiable argument that he most probably was safe with the Cape boys and the dogs.

We walked back to camp, but the first greeting dashed that bolstered hope.

"Where is General Ravenshaw?"

"We haven't seen him."

I went cold with apprehension then and had to persuade myself by going to his tent. It was empty.

The evening was approaching, but I ordered the Cape boys to saddle my own horse and to secure other mounts, as we were going back to search for the lost man. I still felt convinced that Ravenshaw had only been "bushed," but I took my .475 in case it should be needed, and at nine o'clock that night we reached the spot where we had entered the jungle in the afternoon. I dismounted and fired the usual three signal shots; no reply. I then had to admit to Dawson that I too began to fear that Ravenshaw must be dead. The two Cape boys had turned up and said they had seen nothing of the missing man.

But, curiously enough, the Alsatians were still absent.

Tragedy in the Bush

It became obvious to me that wherever Ravenshaw was, there the two dogs would be, for they never stayed in the bush alone but always followed me back to camp. The more I pondered on the disappearance of the Alsatians the more apprehensive I became. Night dropped its curtain, and sent us to uneasy rest. But as soon as it was light Dawson, Fitzroy, and myself, accompanied by ten Cape boys, resumed the search. It will give some idea of the density of the bush when I say that we had gone only five hundred yards after the elephants and had literally combed the spoor and vicinity a dozen times without finding a single trace of the missing man; and yet he could not have wandered far off our trail, for the growth was too difficult to penetrate far in so short a period of time.

We moved forward in extended order, fighting our way through the vicious undergrowth, in the direction we had taken the day before. All that weary day we went backward and forward, but found not a vestige of the General. Late in the afternoon I said to General Dawson that it would be best to return to camp. "I will then send out notices in all directions to ask the farmers to help scour the country."

These notices were circulated as quickly as possible, and in them I requested all my neighbors to gather at the windmill the next morning at eight o'clock. Dawson, Fitzroy, and I were there on the tick of time, and so were forty farmers, accompanied by their native laborers. But the Alsatians were still missing. I showed the farmers the spot where we started from, and once again we set out on our grim quest. At midday we still had found no trace of the missing General.

That final hunt was carried out on organized lines, for I had a whistle with me, and whenever we halted I blew it, and ten minutes later blew it again as a signal for a co-ordinated advance. At one of these halts a well-known farmer, Mr. Walton, was standing beside me, and I told him that I did not think we should be able to find the body until decomposition had set in and the birds directed us. For by now I was convinced that General Ravenshaw was dead. It was but a few minutes after this that my dogs came slowly through the bush. They whined, their tails between their legs. They looked thirsty and famished. I suspected at once that they had been with the General, and had come to find us from our noise because they wanted food. But before feeding them I urged them back into the undergrowth, and we followed them through a perfect thicket of thorn and creeper.

In a bit of a clearing we found him. There was no doubt from the first glance that General Ravenshaw was dead. He was lying face downward and still had his rifle clasped in his hands. I asked everybody to keep away while I made an examination. At once I saw he had not been trampled by an elephant, for all his clothing was intact. Gently I turned the body over, opened the dead soldier's fingers, and took away the rifle, which was loaded. Extracting the cartridges, I looked down the barrel, and saw that not a single shot had been fired. On the General's right cheek was a big dry clot of blood, which I wiped off with a handkerchief, but I knew the wound had been caused merely by a scratch from a thorn bush.

We had to obtain axes to cut away the trees in order to carry the body away from that leafy cloister, and while this was being done a rough litter was made from branches, to carry the body to the wagon road. I pointed out to my companions the marks where the dogs had been lying. The faithful creatures had dug holes in the ground on either side of the body and had lain there with the soldier all the time. How wonderfully loyal Alsatians are!

When we reached the camp I dispatched two wires, one to the magistrate in Port Elizabeth, asking him to come with the police, a doctor, and a coffin. The other message was to Mrs. Ravenshaw, who was staying at Government House, Cape Town. Mrs. Ravenshaw told me later that, before Lady Buxton handed her the telegram, she said, "This is to tell me my husband is dead."

She also informed me that she knew her husband had died four days before she received the message, and, indeed, gave me the approximate time of his passing. Later a post-mortem was held, and the doctor declared the death had been caused by heart failure. We buried him there and then amid the everlasting silence of the bush.

General Dawson told me that he was intensely keen on shooting an elephant before he returned to England, but he was deeply upset by the loss of his friend and did not feel inclined to remain in my camp. I advised him to go to Tanganyika, and gave him a letter to a Native Commissioner who, I knew, would assist him, and arranged for some of my old boys to act as porters. "There are big elephant bulls there," I remember saying to him.

A month or so later I received a letter from Dawson in which he said he had arrived at my camping place, where there was much big elephant spoor, and he felt confident he would enjoy good hunting. To my deep regret, however, two weeks later I received a telegram from the Native Affairs Department informing me that Dawson had died of blackwater fever.

What pitiful luck that both these fine men who had suffered so greatly during the war should come to Africa on holiday and die within three months of their arrival!

CHAPTER NINETEEN

Tempting Death — for the Films

IT WAS a dramatic thought that I had fought and defeated a family of elephants that had held undisputed sway in that bush for thousands of years. For I was convinced they had been isolated, living their own lives independent of any other herds, through untold ages. That, to my view, was why they were tuskless and comparatively small; they had interbred for so many centuries.

You may say that, even though interbreeding might cause physical deterioration, it would not so alter the characteristics of the breed that these animals scarcely had a dozen tusks among the lot of them. This, I think, is the explanation: in all that Addo bush, dense and horrible as it was, there were no big trees, and all the wood was "soft." Through those un-counted years the elephants had not been called upon to use their tusks, and, as is nature's way, if a thing is not used, and thus exercised, it deteriorates until — like the appendix in the human body — it dwindles and eventually dies. I examined a good many dead elephants down there, and in most cases there was not the slightest sign of the growth of tusks; where in any other elephants one found the root-point, here there was nothing but solid bone.

By the way, speaking of tusks, they are not always solid and healthy. You may not see the "illness," but if you detect a little round brown ring on the ivory you can be sure that there are holes inside that render the ivory valueless. The hunter not infrequently comes across an elephant with a broken tusk. This is not the result of disease. It is the outcome either of some tremendous fight or of an accident. When, playing in a river with a rocky bed, the animal has slipped and fallen to its knees, the first part of him to hit the rocky ground is the tusks. I have come across half-lengths and severed tusks myself, in the treacherous beds of African rivers.

One wonders how many thousands of terrible fights have been waged in the dark fastness of the jungles. Seldom does man witness them, but in the Addo I stumbled on the evidence of one on a morning when I was out hunting. There was a stench which grew overpowering as we approached, and I expected every minute to see a dead, putrefying elephant stretched out before me. When we reached the cause of the noxious odor it proved to be not an elephant at all, but two magnificent buffalo cows. The tale was plain to read. The two had fought to the death; their horns were interlocked, and each had pierced her opponent's neck, thus causing death — very likely at the same moment.

Within the year I had finished the Addo job. I was pleased that we had decided to leave a few of the herd — sixteen, in point of fact. I was glad too that we managed to get some records of the animals with the camera. Towards the end, in fact, I engaged a cinema operator, Mr. Joe Albrecht, who took some magnificent shots.

I remember the first time we went out together. We tracked a herd, and I told Albrecht to fix and focus his camera. He had never seen a charging elephant before, and I wondered how he would face up to the business. When he was ready I fired, and down came the thundering herd straight at us. Several passed no more than a couple of paces from us, but Albrecht never budged, and just went on turning the handle. He had pluck, that man — and we had a perfect motion-picture of elephants in full charge. And the very next day we picked up the herd again, and while we took pictures I killed four of the beasts.

With the job done, I thought I should like to substantiate

my theory that the Addo bush animals were a race apart, and looked about to find another herd that were also in some sort of restriction. Eventually, with the approval of the Government, I went to the Knysna Reserve. No shooting had been done here for seventy years; the animals were severely protected. The Forestry Department had been instructed to keep watch so that on my arrival I could be taken at once to the herds.

From Addo I proceeded to George, accompanied by Albrecht, my servants and dogs. At the hotel I heard some of the women in the crowd whispering to one another that they would love to go with me. "Well," said I, "anyone who wishes to come along is quite welcome."

The Chief Forester informed me that we should have to proceed by car into the mountains for seven miles and then walk for another four miles before we reached the kloof where the elephants had been seen two days previously.

After breakfast the next morning, although rain was falling heavily, we all started off, and I am sure that there were as many women as there were men in the party. Among them was a mountaineering excursion from Cape Town consisting of five girls.

The narrow road was bad for the first seven miles, for the ground was slippery, while mud and water splashed us from head to foot. We left the cars at a homestead, and then travelled on foot through slush and morass until five o'clock that afternoon, when we arrived at the edge of a deep kloof covered with great forest trees. I saw yellow-wood trees there that were almost eight feet in diameter and a hundred feet or more in height. These giants mingled with an undergrowth of stately ferns, while sparkling streams rippled away from the kloof, and thus we found a wonderful camping spot against a background of supreme glory. The kloofs were hundreds of feet deep, with precipitous sides — known locally as krantzes —

and often one had to walk as much as a mile before a suitable place for descending could be found.

The forester showed us where he had seen the elephants. I pointed out dense bush quite close to where we were, and told my party to enter the bush and make shelters for the night with the buck-sails and small tents they had brought with them. Then I asked the forester to come with me to the bottom of the kloof in order to discover the trail. We clambered down the cliffs, and when we reached the bottom and had walked about thirty yards I found on the other side elephant paths almost as old as the hills themselves. Not a tree nor a blade of grass grew along these paths, and I saw the spoor of elephants that had passed there that morning, travelling eastward along the line of the cliffs.

"If we follow the spoor for a mile or so shall we be able to find a way up the cliffs again?" I asked.

"Yes," the forester answered. "I know of a practical ascent a mile along the kloof."

Tracing the tracks for five hundred yards, we came on a dead elephant calf, three feet high, which had died a few days previously. This was the first dead elephant I had ever seen that had died a natural death in natural surroundings. There were no wounds on the little beast; moreover, he was in a reserve where no one was allowed to shoot, and it was obvious the Dumbo must have devoured some substance that had created severe intestinal trouble.

We had a terrible climb that night, for we had to scramble up cliffs three hundred feet high on our hands and knees in soaking rain. When we reached the camp we found that half of the elephant enthusiasts had already gone to bed, for all were dead tired. It was a damp and misty atmosphere, and we had scarcely been able to see anything, but the next morning we were pleasantly surprised as the mist rose above the trees. We sat on the edge of the krantzes looking to the north, and gazed on dense forests split by a strip of open land fifty yards wide, and, I suppose, over a thousand yards long, in which the grass was stunted, so that we could see everything that moved in that space. As we stood admiring the forests, with their titanic trees, and a huge land-slide on the opposite cliffs, I observed seven elephants crossing the open strip at the far end. I pointed out the great beasts to the excursionists, and they were thrilled at their first sight of wild elephants.

At once I began to discuss making a cinematograph film of the elephants, and proposed to Albrecht and the Chief Forester that we should descend into the opening and make for a point where the elephants had disappeared into the bush. We could find a suitable spot for the camera, and I would then remain with Albrecht while the forester, my two dogs, and the boys proceeded to the spot where we had seen the elephants go. They were then to let the dogs loose. I knew that as soon as the hounds disappeared and disturbed the elephants they would clear as fast as they could along their old path. Elephants never make new paths, but keep to their old thoroughfares, the road of the centuries. Our camera was to be planted in the middle of the path, and I was confident that the elephants would dash towards us. Just before we left I told the excursionists to stand on the edge of the cliffs, so that they would have a ring-side view of all that happened.

Down we went. The Chief Forester took the dogs and set off. When they reached the spot where the elephants had entered the jungle they loosed the hounds. At once the dogs picked up the spoor, and scarcely a minute later the shrill sound of barking reached us. Next I heard the elephants, and then came the sound of breaking trees as the great beasts approached the spot where we were standing in wait with the cameras.

Fortune favored us. The leader of the herd was a huge bull, who suddenly appeared thirty yards away. He put up his ears, raised his trunk, and charged. I hit him, at a range of twenty paces, but my bullet did not turn him; he still crashed forward. Albrecht stuck to his camera. I had to shoot again, and this time put a bullet in his ear which dropped him.

But now the excitement was rising, for the dogs were chasing the rest of the herd towards us. While I was still concentrating on the first bull the party yelled, "Look out!" I turned and saw another bull charging straight towards the camera. I let drive and gave him a bullet in the head which dropped him, but it was not a fatal shot, and he quickly rose. The next time I fired at his brain, and he fell dead. We watched him then in wonder, for he had fallen on a slope and the carcase began to roll, and over and over it went down the hill. It was a weird and terrific spectacle to see such a huge animal rolling helplessly, taking trees and branches with him, until finally the immense body came to rest against a monster tree.

The spectators on the cliffs now began to scramble down, and came tearing along to have a close-up view of the elephants. When all had taken photographs I indicated a good camping site under the trees. All our kit was brought down, and we parked ourselves fifty yards away from the elephants. I knew it would take at least three days to prepare the specimens. In order to practice taxidermy in the wild, I used a large chart on which an elephant was drawn to scale, and when we measured each part of the mammoth anatomy we would jot down the size on the drawing; and in that way, after the elephant was skinned, etc., we should know its exact dimensions, so that the great animal mass could be accurately reconstructed for the museum.

The Chief Forester took all the measurements, while I jotted them on the chart. The height of this elephant, from the foot to the top of the shoulder, was 12 feet 6 inches. To my knowledge there was not at that time another twelve-and-a-half-foot elephant in any museum in the world. The length of the elephant, from the tip of his trunk to the end of his tail, was 22 feet 6 inches. I was satisfied — for I had proved my theory regarding the Addo elephants. Was it not patent that the two types were entirely different, and that the Addo elephants had degenerated owing to the lack of trees, while those in the parkland of Knysna Forest had retained the characteristics of the centuries and were of the same type as all others in Africa?

After the elephants had been skinned and their hides put out to dry I made arrangements with the magistrate and the Forestry Department to transport the specimens from the cliffs, as soon as ·they were complete, for dispatch to Cape Town. The largest elephant was stuffed, and now stands in the Cape Museum. The film proved a tremendous success, and was shown all over the Union and in other countries as well. So true to life was it that on the film a blotch appeared on the elephant where the bullet had entered.

And so my hunting excursions in the Cape Province terminated. They had provided me with much excitement, interest, and substantial remuneration. I bade good-bye to those majestic forests and mountains of Knysna, and returned to Nylstroom, in my own land.

But not for long.

The film I had taken in the Addo bush, and in the Knysna Forest, did not make a reel long enough to provide a whole evening's entertainment, so I decided to complete the picture by organizing a lion hunt, in which I hoped to portray a charging lion. I therefore went to Pretoria, and, since unfortunately I could not get the services of Albrecht, I had to advertise for another cameraman. One morning an applicant arrived at my hotel and introduced himself as Mr. Fritz.[1] He was, I should say, twenty-seven years of age, of fair complexion, and robust build. From his speech I knew at once

[1] This name is fictitious.

that he was a German. I told him I was proceeding to the Sabie
Game Reserve in order to obtain motion-pictures of a lion
charging, and that I proposed to kill the lion at a ten-foot
range when the animal rushed me. To obtain such a picture I
explained that the camera would have to be set and focused,
and to make a comprehensive film I should have to be no
farther than seven yards from the camera.

"Oh, that is quite all right; I am a good cameraman, and I
am afraid of nothing," Herr Fritz at once ejaculated.

"Good," said I, "and what salary do you require?"

"Well," he said, "forty-eight pounds a month and everything found would be reasonable."

This was in 1921, when camera operators were almost unob-
tainable in the Union, and I therefore decided to engage the
man, and at once we left Pretoria for the reserve.

The Administrator of the Transvaal had given me permission to enter the Kruger National Park, and to carry out the
necessary photographic work which I desired. He had, too,
instructed Colonel de Jager, a game ranger at Kaapmuiden, to
give me all the assistance he could in my quest for lions. The
Colonel had arranged for us to stay in his bungalow just across
the Crocodile river in the reserve. And now a big obstacle
presented itself — we should have to trek for two days by
wagon to reach the lion country. Although there were plenty
of oxen in the district, they were not permitted to cross the
Crocodile river, and it was impossible to proceed by car, for
the country consisted of broken bush, and there were no roads
of any description. I was told that if I could obtain donkeys I
could cross the river with them, and eventually I had to send
to Barberton and obtain a wagon with a span of donkeys.

There were no fords at the Crocodile river in the locality
where we were, and Colonel de Jager told me we should have
to trek along the bank for two days before we reached a spot
where the water was only four feet deep, and there we could

cut down the banks of the river and make a drift for the wagon to cross. Just before we reached the Crocodile river de Jager sent two runners who were instructed to ascertain where there were lions, and when they located them to report at once. At nine o'clock the police boys returned and said that they had found two kills. One was a bush-buck and the other a zebra, around which were five lions. We seized the camera, and set off post-haste to the zebra kill. The lions were there all right, but the moment they saw us they trotted off into the bush.

Colonel de Jager had several mongrel dogs with him, one of which was a three-quarter-breed bull-terrier, named Bodkers, and a rattling good hound he was, too. I had my two Alsatians with me. Colonel de Jager endeavored to make his dogs chase the lions, but they just shivered with their tails between their legs, and would not move; I therefore unleashed my dogs, which were well-nigh uncontrollable by now, and when I loosed them they shot off like rockets on the trail of the lions.

"We will stay here until we hear the dogs barking," I said, "and then we can make straight for the pride."

Near by was a high hill scarred by a kloof, and after we had waited for five minutes we heard fierce barking from the direction of the kloof. We walked straight towards it, and when we were fifty yards away I told the rest of the party to remain there while I advanced by myself, for I could hear one lion in a deep donga roaring fiercely and almost making the ground shake, while the dogs barked like furies. As I stepped forward to the edge of the donga the police boys yelled out to Colonel de Jager, "Don't let him go, bass. The lion will kill him." When I reached the edge I looked down into the eyes of the lion, for he was standing in the bottom of the donga. The banks were twelve feet high and very steep, so that the lion could not reach me with a jump, although he endeavored to do so.

My two dogs were on guard, one faced the lion's left shoulder and the other his hindquarters, and both the hounds nipped at the King of Beasts and worried him. They were clever enough to keep out of reach of the lion's paw, for they seemed to know instinctively that one smack from those terrific pads would have crushed their skulls.

When I realized that the Alsatians were quite safe I called to the others to come and view the lion. We all stood on the edge of the donga and admired the beast, for he was indeed a magnificent animal, possessed of a gorgeous black mane. As he roared we picked up pebbles and threw them into his wide-open mouth, trying to incense him to tackle me while the camera was being set. He, however, simply spat the stones out, and continued to roar. We exposed approximately a hundred feet of film which, when developed, showed the lion's teeth and mouth with great clarity, and made a splendid picture of animal fury. That, however, was not enough, for I wanted to film the King of Beasts charging. The donga was very steep, but I noticed that forty yards away an old game path zig-zagged down the sides, and I suggested to Fritz that I should descend the donga by way of the game path. We would, I said, place the camera there, focus the whole bank in the lens, and when everything was in readiness I would clamber into the donga, where the lion would at once tackle me.

Just as I was climbing down the bank, my wife (I had married again) said she wanted to come down with me. Although she had no rifle, she wished to accompany me, and I agreed.

The moment we landed at the bottom of the donga, on a big, flat rock, which was six feet long and four feet wide, the lion jerked himself loose from my dogs, gave a terrific roar, and bounded towards me. He came at me like a rocket — so fast, indeed, that I could hardly see his paws on the ground. I had my .475 rifle, with finger on trigger, ready, and the moment the lion was within ten feet of us he sprang, and simultaneously I fired. The beast crumpled up and crashed to the ground about two feet away from us, while his head struck the rock on which my wife and I were standing. I lowered my rifle and waited, but there was no movement in legs or paws, and I knew that he was dead.

I looked round at my wife and saw her calmly standing there, smiling and unperturbed. But Herr Fritz was forty yards away and running for dear life. I do not know where he thought he was going, but there was no doubt in my mind as to where he should go. After a while he slowed up, turned round, and shouted, "I am sorry, sir, I didn't take it." Thus, for all our trouble, we had no film! For the moment I could quite cheerfully have throttled him.

We examined the lion, and found that the bullet had entered the brain right between the eyes. The skin was stuffed, and was to be seen at the house of the late Colonel Mentz in South Africa.

The cinema-man's failure to obtain that picture cost me a good two hundred pounds, for I spent nearly three months in the reserve before I could induce another lion to charge me under such dramatic circumstances and ideal photographic conditions. We went out early every morning, often not returning until late in the evening, but our quests were fruitless.

We saw lions practically every day, but the moment they saw us they would turn and run for their lives. We sent natives out one morning as usual to look for spoor, and one of my boys came back and told us that he had seen a big leopard which had one foot entrapped in a small iron game-trap, and that when he had reached the animal it had threatened to charge him. Knowing that a leopard puts up a pretty good fight, we set off immediately with the camera. After we had travelled for about an hour we came to a large river, which had a number of reed islands in the centre. Within fifty yards of the river the boys indicated a thick patch of reeds as the one in which the leopard had been trapped.

I told the party with me to stay, and I walked to the spot. I went in carefully, opening the reeds slowly, and suddenly came upon a big male leopard right in front of me. He snarled and moved forward to tackle me, but as there was no camera available I quickly returned to the others. Trapped animals are far more dangerous than others, for, although people imagine that the trap itself is a severe handicap, in actual fact that is often not the case. Traps are not always fastened to a tree, and in consequence an animal frequently charges with the trap attached to its legs, and the pain caused by the jaws of the trap renders an animal so ensnared more ferocious than usual.

To set the camera it was found that we should have to cross the river, otherwise the sun would be shining directly into the lens. A suitable crossing was discovered, and we reached the bank directly opposite the trapped leopard. There was a big, flat rock in front of us, and beyond that was the river-bed; on the other side of the river were a few scattered trees and the patch of reeds where the leopard was at bay. We placed the camera on a rock and focused the whole of the foreground. My plan was to walk right up to the leopard, tease him, and then when he chased me I would run towards the camera, while Fritz took the photograph. The rest of the party declared that it was too risky an undertaking, and that I should in all probability be killed — but that, after all, was my own affair.

"What I want you people to do," I said, "is to give me a shout when the leopard jumps, and then I will turn and shoot." Fritz now informed me that the camera was ready and that I could proceed, while the rest of the folk remained about ten yards behind the operator.

With my .475 all set I walked towards the spot where we supposed the animal lay. But while we had been preparing the camera the leopard had changed his position, and actually had been stalking me! I had gone only half-way when he gave a tremendous snarl that was half a belch and half a roar, and charged. I turned and ran as hard as I could towards the camera. The iron which the leopard had on his foot was very light and hampered him but little. He came at me like an arrow loosed from a bow.

"He has got you! He has got you!" I heard the people on the rock shout. I could almost feel the great cat scratch against my heels, but I continued running as hard as I could. I was confident that he could not kill me instantaneously, and even if I did receive a few wounds I was determined not to shoot him until he actually tackled me. I dashed on about fifteen yards past the camera, when the leopard, suddenly observing Fritz, abandoned me and charged the cinema-man. Fritz fled, but as he ran round the camera the handle hooked him firmly in the pocket of his riding-breeches, and the instrument toppled over on top of him. It weighed nearly a hundred pounds, and pinned Fritz to the ground, while the leopard jumped on top of the tangled mass made up of the terrified man and the cinema machine.

Instead of mauling Fritz, the leopard began to chew the camera, so I rushed back with the rifle and as I passed I poked the leopard with the barrel. The leopard turned and tackled me, and as I jumped aside my servant Nacosia (who had my other rifle) fired, and nearly shot me. The bullet whistled towards me, struck the ground a few paces in front of me and blinded me with sand. By this time Fritz had freed himself from the camera by ripping his breeches from the pocket to the bottom, and scrambled to safety saying over and over again, "What a narrow shave! What a narrow shave!" There was no one to take the film, for Fritz was completely unnerved, and so I had to kill the leopard. Once again a wonderfully thrilling picture had been missed — the films had not been taken, and momentarily I wished that Fritz, and not the leopard, was dead.

Two days later one of the runners who had left early in the morning returned just before noon, and told us that higher up on the same river he had seen three large lions lying under a tree. Taking the dogs, we sallied forth post-haste, but when we reached the spot the lions had disappeared. Thereupon I loosed the dogs, and we soon heard them barking near the river. Fifty yards from the bank I told the party to stay where they were, while I reconnoitred the lions. The banks of the river were lined with dense bush and date-palms. The moment I reached the edge of the river a lioness spotted me and rushed in full charge. Just as she was about to make the death-spring I fired, hit her between the eyes, and split her skull as though it had been cleft by an axe. She fell as dead as a door-nail, but as I had shot her suddenly to protect myself no picture was taken.

I now called the party to come along. The two other lions had cleared off into the bush, which was a mass of date-palms. Here the Alsatians had singled out a very large black-maned lion, but we could not take photographs, for the bush was too dense and the dogs could not chivvy the lion out of it. Several times I entered the lair to see if I could brush aside some of the vegetation, but the lion itself was not visible, and I could only see the movements of the trees where the beast lay.

We now decided to set fire to the bush and the oily date-palms, which burn quickly, in order to drive the lion out into the parkland country which adjoined. As soon as the flames began to lick the bush the lion dashed away, and I put the dogs on chains, for I was afraid they would chase the beast too far. Then I followed the spoor, leaving the rest of the party on the bank of the river. Five hundred yards farther on I came to burned grass and lost the spoor. Here was a fairly open space on which grew short, stunted bushes about three feet high. I searched diligently for the continuation of the spoor and travelled in all directions four or five times before I suddenly spotted the lion. He lay about thirty yards away between two little bushes, and had taken full advantage of nature's protective environment. The bushes were burned on top, and the lion's black mane just showed above the trees; it looked for all the world as though there were three trees growing together.

The lion crouched between the bushes peering at us, but only a well-trained bushman's eyes could detect his presence. I pointed out his camouflaged form to the two runners, and remarked, "We have passed up and down four times, and he has been lying watching us all the time." Immediately they wanted to run, but I stopped them and said if they cleared out the lion would tackle us, and therefore the wisest plan was to walk back to our friends. I sent one boy ahead to summon the rest of the party, and walked casually away. The other boy I told not to look at the lion, as I felt convinced that if we just ignored him he would lie quiet.

Ten minutes later the other members of the safari arrived with the camera, and I asked them all to "find the lion," as though it was a picture puzzle. They stared hard everywhere, and, although they looked straight at the animal, they could not see him. When I pointed him out they could just make out his eyes, but so wonderfully was he concealed that they could not pick out his shape.

We soon fixed the camera, and I then told the boys that the moment I threw a stone at the lion they were to let the dogs loose. When Fritz was ready I hurled the pebble, which fell between the lion's front paws. The beast jumped up and charged at us, but the dogs intercepted him half-way. Bodkers was the first to reach him. The lion grabbed him and crumpled him up so that I thought every bone in his body would be broken, and Bodkers remained lying there as still as death. Next His Majesty tackled my Alsatians, and then rushed at us.

Urging Fritz to hang on, we were at long last able to secure the film of a lion charging. Just before the animal reached us I laid him low with a bullet that entered the corner of his eye and penetrated his brain. This skin too is to be seen in the house of Colonel Mentz. We returned to Pretoria with the photographs, which were developed and printed in the African Film Company's studios at Killarney, a suburb of Johannesburg. We exhibited the picture in the Pretoria Town Hall for five performances, and every night we had a full-to-capacity house.

"For to admire an' for to see." Kipling's line comes to mind as I look back on my long and not uneventful life. For the *leit-motiv* of it all has been just that — to adventure over the next hill-crest or around the next corner. After the film incidents I did "settle down" temporarily, urged largely by the fact that our children needed educational facilities. I was fortunate in being able to mix that duty with one or two jobs that suited my hunter's mood. For a time I shot wild animals — lions, leopards, wild dogs, and so on — which had been killing an average of fifteen hundred head of cattle every year on one of the largest farms in the whole of Africa — the Nuanetsi Ranch, in Southern Rhodesia. While I was there a governess undertook the education of the youngsters, and I did some shooting, for which I was well paid — so much a head for the beasts which were carrying out this large-scale slaughter.

Incidentally, I got nothing for crocodiles, because some local man had discovered a method of killing off dozens a night. He would sit on the bank of a river and flash an ordinary pocket torch over the surface. The crocs, who are as inquisitive as domestic cows, would float to the surface to see what the light was and would be promptly shot as a reward for their curiosity. Apparently they never learned.

Then the manager of the ranch, Mr. Dreyer, whom I had known in German East Africa, told me that the Bubi section was without a manager, and offered me that area to control. Thus passed a happy five years; but by then the children needed more civilized surroundings — better education, and others of their kind to mix with — and so the Man of the Bush became a humble resident in the Golden City of Johannesburg. After that there was a space when I tried industry, running a cartage business and doing motor transport. But I tired of it, went back to my old home, and developed certain properties I owned there. Life was interesting enough while I was busy, but I have no taste for locusts, and I found that the urge to travel was as strong as it was in those far-off days when, as a boy, I heard the whips crack about the line of transport. I knew I must push out again. First, however, I was persuaded to tell this story of my life, thinking it might light unknown trails to the interest of those who knew them not.

Now it is finished, and I put aside the unaccustomed pen with some relief to take my more familiar Jeffries and go again to the wilds where the big animals roam, leaving behind, unregretfully, the noisy strife we call civilization.

Index

Index

Index

Chibalo, Chief, 56
Chicago Gaiko Mine, 37
Chicova, lost mines of, 77
Chikunda, tribe, 80
Chitendavunga, 89
Chukunda, 89
Chulesi, river, 178
Churchill, Winston S., broadcast by, 24
Chyawa, Paramount Chief, 87-95;
    murder of, 93
Coco-nuts, 20
Coerney Station, 210, 227
Crocodile, river, 239-240
Crocodiles, 65, 67, 78, 137-139; eggs
    of, 64; nests of, 137

Da Conia, 158
Da Costa, 177-178
D'Arcy, Miss, 222
Dar-es-Salaam, 22, 128-129, 131, 136,
    206
Dawson, General, 225, 227, 229, 231
de Jager, Colonel, 239-240
de la Rey, Miss, 181
Delgado, Cape, 99, 139
De Waal, Sir Frederick, 208-209, 225
Dhows, 27
Diempe, 90; village of, 93
Dooner, Captain, 196
Dreyer, 248
Drums, native, 50
Durban, 19, 181-182, 209
Dysentery, 41

East Africa, 27
East coast, African, 47
Eland, 97-98
Elephants, 17, 54, 72-73, 109-110,
    114, 116-121, 129, 131-136, 139,
    148-150, 153, 155, 158-159, 207-
    208, 213-216, 225, 234-238;
    total bag of, 42; how Pygmies

Elephants, *continued*
    hunt, 116; age of, 131; supersti-
    tions connected with, 133; track-
    ing of, 132-133; peculiarities of,
    142-143; the "Iron Herd," 143;
    poaching exploits for, 158-159;
    telepathic communication of,
    162; baby, 217; feeding, in cap-
    tivity, 220-221; milk of, 220-221;
    instinct of, 221-222; scent of,
    226; cinema shots of, 233; meas-
    urements of, 237-238
Emtapiri, river, 178
Engelbrecht, 195-196

Fever, 50, 80, 127, 136
Fish, electric, 139-140
Fishing, native methods of, 137, 139
Fitzroy, 225, 227, 229
Flying crickets, 77
Fort Johnston, 180
Fort Valentine, 178
Fort Victoria, 34
Fourie, Philip, 219
Fritz, 238-239, 241-247
Fusiliers, 25th Royal, 193, 195

Gahiki, Paramount Chief, 127
Gazelle, 42
George, Cape Province, 234
German East Africa, 101, 121, 157
Germans seize author's cattle, 128;
    steal author's farm, 157
Gold belts, 37
Goliath, H.M.S., 19, 24, 182
Gorillas, 114, 118-121; encounter
    with, 118
Grant, James A., 121 n.
"Grauwfametif," 35
Greener shot-gun, 66
Guide to British South Africa Com-
    pany's Forces, 36

252

Index

Index

254

Index

Index